Getting Involved With God

GETTING INVOLVED WITH GOD

Rediscovering the Old Testament

ELLEN F. DAVIS

A COWLEY PUBLICATIONS BOOK

Lanham, Chicago, New York, Toronto, and Plymouth, UK

A COWLEY PUBLICATIONS BOOK

ROWMAN & LITTLEFIELD PUBLISHERS, INC.

Published in the United States of America
by Rowman & Littlefield Publishers, Inc.
A wholly owned subsidiary of The Rowman & Littlefield Publishing Group, Inc.
4501 Forbes Boulevard, Suite 200, Lanham, Maryland 20706
www.rowmanlittlefield.com

Estover Road
Plymouth PL6 7PY
United Kingdom

British Library Cataloguing in Publication Information Available

An earlier version of "Desirable Discipline" appeared in *The Living Pulpit* (Summer
2000). "Serving in the Shadows" was first published in the Yale Divinity School
publication *Reflections* (Winter/Spring 1994).
Scripture quotations other than the author's translation are taken from *The New Revised
Standard Version* of the Bible, © 1989 by the Division of Christian Education of the
National Council of the Churches of Christ in the United States of America. Used by
permission.

Cover design by Vicki Black and Peggy Parker; author photograph by Alexander Dorr
Cover art: *Noah and the Dove (1976), Exodus from Egypt (1976), A Psalm of David
(1980), and Joseph (1974)* by Kopel Gurwin (1923–1990).

Library of Congress Cataloging-in-Publication Data

Davis, Ellen F.
   Getting involved with God : rediscovering the Old Testament / Ellen F. Davis.
   p. cm.
   Includes bibliographical references.
   ISBN 1-56101-197-5 (alk. paper)
   1. Bible. O. T.—Introductions. 2. Bible. O. T.—Theology. I. Title
BS1140.3 .D38 2001
221.6'1—dc21   2001042308

Printed in the United States of America.

☉™ The paper used in this publication meets the minimum requirements of
American National Standard for Information Sciences—Permanence of
Paper for Printed Library Materials, ANSI/NISO Z39.48-1992.

For Morley, Nico, Nicolaas, Paiter, Isaac, and Ezra
our new generations of faith

CONTENTS

Introduction 1

I. PAIN AND PRAISE:
THE PSALMS AS COMMON PRAYER

1. Improving Our Aim
   Praying the Psalms 7
2. "With My Tears I Melt My Mattress"
   The Psalms of Lament 14
3. But Surely Not Those!
   The Cursing Psalms 23
4. "Lamenting into Dancing"
   The Psalms of Praise. 30

II. THE COST OF LOVE

5. "I've Got to Turn Aside"
   The Burning Bush 45
6. "Take Your Son"
   The Binding of Isaac. 50
7. "The One Whom My Soul Loves"
   The Song of Songs. 65

III. THE ART OF LIVING WELL
8. Wise Ignorance
  The Book of Proverbs 91
9. Simple Gifts
  The Book of Ecclesiastes 104
10. The Sufferer's Wisdom
  The Book of Job. 121

IV. HABITS OF THE HEART
11. Desirable Discipline
  Proverbs 8. 147
12. A Fool for Love
  Exodus 33. 153
13. "Like Grass I'm Dried Up"
  Psalm 102. 160
14. Voluntary Heartbreak
  Psalm 51. 168
15. Serving in the Shadows
  Isaiah 49. 176

V. TORAH OF THE EARTH
16. "Good-Faith Springs Up from the Earth":
  Learning Ecology From the Bible 185
17. Greed and Prophecy 202
  Numbers 11

ACKNOWLEDGMENTS

THIS BOOK DRAWS UPON lectures and sermons delivered over a period of fourteen years. Looking back to the beginning of that period, I wish to thank the people of St. James Episcopal Church, Manhattan for showing me that "ordinary churchgoers" are eager to engage the biggest and most difficult questions of biblical theology; thus they fostered the style of teaching represented here.

This is a book which owes its existence to an editor. Cynthia Shattuck conceived the idea for it, and she made the considerable effort to discover its outlines hidden in a stack of lecture notes. Through many years of friendship, she has gently pressed me toward a writing style that is less dense. Through the several years during which this book fitfully took form, she both waited patiently for me to move and guided my movements when they were awkward. I thank her and the staff of Cowley Publications for their excellent work and their graciousness.

The Virginia Theological Seminary granted me a sabbatical leave to complete the writing. I am grateful to the staff of the Bishop Payne Library, and to Shawn McDermott especially, for efficient and cheerful help; to my students and also my Dean, Martha Horne, for their genuine interest. It is a privilege to enjoy the strong supports of home along with the freedom of a sabbatical.

As always, greatest thanks are due to Dwayne Huebner for his consistent generosity toward a wife for whom writing is both painstaking labor and essential recreation. This book is dedicated to our children and grandchildren.

All translations of the biblical text (unless otherwise noted) are the author's. Her references to verse numbers follow the enumeration in the Hebrew Bible, which may differ (minus one) from English translations. Where references alone are cited in the text, verse numbers refer to those given in the New Revised Standard Version *of the Bible.*

INTRODUCTION

THIS IS A BOOK about getting, and staying, involved with God—what it takes, what it costs, what it looks and feels like, why anyone would want to do it anyway. It is at the same time a book about reading the Old Testament as a source of Good News and guidance for our life with God. The key piece of Good News that the Old Testament communicates over and over again is that God is involved with us, deeply and irrevocably so. We hear that message affirmed in many different voices and in shifting moods: in the voices of the psalmists crying out to God across the full range of human emotions, from grief to joy, from uncontained rage to dumbfounded gratitude; and also in the voice of God, spoken through poets, storytellers, prophets, and teachers. As it turns out, God's life is as complex as our own—and it is so, precisely because God's life is bound up inextricably with ours.

This book commends a style of spiritually engaged reading that is, I think, largely unfamiliar to Christians. I offer it as an alternative to two more common ways of approaching the Old Testament. The first, common among conservative Christians, is to read it chiefly as prophesying the birth, death, and resurrection of Jesus Christ. In many cases, those who take this approach also find moral teachings useful for Christians in some parts of the Old Testament (the Ten Commandments, Proverbs, and a few psalms) and a straightforward account of history in other parts (Genesis, for example); the rest is largely ignored. A second option, more common among liberal Christians, is to assume that wherever the Old Testament is not boring (which is most places), it is morally deficient. That is, it represents a distinctly inferior moral sensibility. Those who take this view are not inclined to read the Old Testament at all—nor, if they are clergy, to preach from it. It is assumed that everything necessary for salvation appears in the New Testament, in a conveniently abbreviated form.

My approach differs from both. I am convinced that the Old Testament is necessary for Christians. But what I am exploring here is not its prophetic function or even its moral teachings—if by that we mean a set of inflexible rules about what we should or should not do. Rather, I am looking for what the Old Testament tells us about intimate life with God. Ever since the second century the church has maintained that the New Testament does not by itself tell us everything we need to know about that.[1] The reason Christians need to find the Good News in the Old Testament is that the New Testament writers always presuppose the Old Testament— and not only in the places where they specifically cite it for support. Much more often, they assume that their audience is already familiar with and benefitting from its instruction. Where the Old Testament treats an aspect of the spiritual life to their satisfaction, then the New Testament writers rely upon that older and still-authoritative treatment, as did Jesus himself. In other words, the Old Testament is their theological base, "not authoritative only where it is *referred* to in the New, but also when it is *deferred* to."[2]

The five sections of this book constitute an unsystematic introduction to the Old Testament for those who want to get involved with God. If there is a secret to getting involved with God through the pages of scripture, then perhaps it is this: *turn the pages slowly.* One of my students in an introductory Old Testament course once said, "When I started this course, I thought that my problem was that I read too slowly. Now I realize that I read too fast." Our reading style reflects our culture's general admiration for speed. Modern novels have taught recreational readers to skim for plot. Many of us have to read for our jobs, and we pride ourselves on how rapidly we can move through vast quantities of print. But the Bible discourages us from making mileage a measure of success. In many cases, its riches are perceptible only to those who move slowly, like mushroom hunters, peering closely where at first there appears to be nothing at all to see. Almost always it is useful to linger over a word or a phrase that seems strangely chosen. So the essays and sermons here frequently pose the question, "Why does the Bible say it this way, instead of the way we might have expected?" For it is by means of words that the Bible performs its revelatory function. An unexpected word can jar us into contemplating new possibilities about how things really are. An ambiguous word jogs our minds onto a completely different track. Often when reading one portion of scripture, we run across words that echo another passage. Thus the biblical writers lead us subtly to make connections—between events in the text and likewise between events in our lives—that we had never previously imagined.

This kind of reading takes much time and patience, because we are in fact learning a whole new way of thinking and being in the world. This fact is obscured by the notion, current in universities and some seminaries, that biblical interpretation is a "science." Acquiring scientific knowledge

4

and skill may be arduous, but it generally does not make a fundamental change in the way we look at reality. Yet when we acquire the habit of reading scripture in a spiritually engaged way, we do look at the world in a profoundly different way. It is not that the Bible paints a glossy picture, as many people—mostly those who have never read it— believe. No, it shows us our familiar world, with difficulties all too real, and sometimes intractable. The Bible is relentlessly realistic about the world and our situation in it. It does not pretend that things are better than they are, nor entice us to imagine that we can transcend the difficulties through some kind of spiritual superiority, innate or acquired. Nonetheless, a radical change happens as we read deeply. In the sixteenth century, John Calvin, one of the deepest scripture readers of all time, aptly compared the Bible to a pair of spectacles: it enables us to see things we could not see at all before, to find meaning in what was an unidentifiable blur. We can see where we are. The world itself may not be any safer, but our place in it is more secure, our movement through it more certain. If reading scripture well is like putting on a pair of glasses, then the best thing about it is that when we talk, we can see clearly who is out there. So this book begins with our talking to God.

Notes

1. The first heresy identified by the church was Marcionism, the view that the Old Testament does not reflect true knowledge of God and is therefore not the sacred scripture of the church.

2. Christopher Seitz, *Word Without End: The Old Testament as Abiding Theological Witness* (Grand Rapids: Eerdmans, 1998), 222.

PART ONE

PAIN AND PRAISE

The Psalms as Common Prayer

THE PSALMS MODEL ways of talking to God that are honest, yet not obvious—at least, they are not obvious to modern Christians. They may guide our first steps toward deeper involvement with God, because the Psalms give us a new possibility for prayer; they invite full disclosure. They enable us to bring into our conversation with God feelings and thoughts that most of us think we need to get rid of before God will be interested in hearing from us. The point of the shocking psalms is not to sanctify what is shameful (for example, the desire for sweet revenge) or to make us feel better about parts of ourselves that stand in need of change. Rather, the Psalms teach us that profound change happens always in the presence of God. Over and over they attest to the reality that when we open our minds and hearts fully to the God who made them, then we open ourselves, whether we know it or not, to the possibility of being transformed beyond our imagining.

CHAPTER ONE

IMPROVING OUR AIM

Praying the Psalms

I BEGIN WITH the Psalms "because they are there"—and not just within the covers of the Hebrew Bible. Start noticing, and you will see that the Psalms are everywhere. They are there in the New Testament, quoted even more frequently than the Prophets. They are there in worship: a snippet or more of the Psalms appears in nearly every traditional Catholic and Protestant service. Psalms structure our whole way of talking to God, whether we know it or not: "O Lord, open Thou our lips.... And our mouth shall show forth Thy praise"—that is Psalm 51 (v. 17), not Luther or Cranmer. The Psalms are there, all of them, in missals and Protestant prayer books; the Psalter is the one book of the Bible to which, it seems, prayerful Christians require immediate daily access. They are even there at the back of my tiny traveler's edition of the New Testament, the kind that evangelistic shopkeepers distribute free to their customers.

Of course, there is a reason why they are ubiquitous, and why we should begin with them: because the Psalms are the single best guide to the spiritual life currently in print. They will likely still be on the shelf long after everything else in the spirituality section of the bookstore has gone out of print. Anything you could learn from the other books is already there, at least in kernel form, in the Psalter. The Psalms are a guide to prayer, but they are also a corrective to a lot of common misconceptions about religion and prayer. If we read and pray the Psalms, and really listen to what they say, to what we are saying when we pray them, then our ideas about prayer will change. These biblical prayers expose the hollow sentimentality that often masquerades as prayer, the dangerous falsity of things we have heard—and maybe even thought ourselves—about how we ought to think and talk when God is around. Things like this: *God does not have any use for our anger;* we must have already forgiven our enemy before God will listen to our prayer. Another false notion of prayer: Since we are people of hope (that part is true, but now comes the false corollary), *there is no place for despair or fear in the Christian life.* Or this instruction, which has probably quenched more prayer than any other: *You must never, ever be mad at God.* It is largely because of ideas such as these that many of us do not pray more often or more deeply.

The problem with all these notions of prayer is that we cannot have an intimate relationship with someone to whom we cannot speak honestly—that is, someone to whom we cannot show our ugly side, or those large clay feet of ours. We in this culture are all psychologically astute enough to know that honest, unguarded speaking is essential to the health of family life or close friendship. But do we realize that the same thing applies to our relationship with God? That is what the Psalms are about: speaking our mind honestly and fully before God. The Psalms are a kind of First Amendment for the faithful. They guarantee us complete freedom of speech before God, and then (something no secular constitution would ever do) they give us a detailed model of how to exercise that freedom, even up to its dangerous limits, to the very brink of rebellion.

For the Psalms are not all rhapsodies of praise, proclaiming that God is enthroned in heaven and all is right with the world. Many of them suggest that in fact there is a great deal wrong with the world, and they demand that God do something about it. They are at times embarrassingly unsublime. Take, for instance, the psalmist's pious wish that his enemies would melt like a slug on a hot road (Psalm 58:8). Yet because these unedifying outbursts are in the Bible, they come to us as the Word of God. And that irony brings us to the most important thing about the Psalms: they are undisguisedly human utterances. The Psalter is, in fact, the only part of the Bible that is clearly formulated as human speech, packaged ready to be put directly into our mouths. All the rest of the Bible represents God's speaking to us—directly, in the Prophets; or less directly through the history of Israel, or the gospel narratives, or the wise sayings of Proverbs. Only the Psalms are formulated as prayer, as human words to God. Yet because they are part of the Bible, we understand them also as God's word to us—or better, the Psalms are God's word *in* us. To paraphrase Paul in the letter to the Romans (8:26), the Psalms are the Spirit of God speaking through us, helping us to pray when we do not know how to pray as we ought, which is most of the time.

So the Psalms call for honest speech, but honesty is not everything in an intimate relationship. We must also speak wisely, at least some of the time. And if we attend to the Psalms patiently and deeply, they will teach us wisdom in prayer. It is no coincidence that the first psalm is a wisdom psalm; probably it came out of ancient Israel's academies of higher learning. Its words provide a context for understanding everything that follows:

9

Privileged is the person
who has not walked in the council of the wicked,
nor stood in the path of sinners,
nor settled in the settlement of scorners.
Rather in the Teaching [*tôrah*] of the LORD is
his delight,
and in his Teaching he murmurs day and night.
(1:1-2)

The first psalm gives us a picture of what happens to the person who "murmurs" these godly teachings day and night:

And he is like a tree
planted along streams of water,
which yields its fruit in due season,
and its leaf does not wither,
and everything he does prospers. (1:3)

"Everything he does prospers"—this is an extravagant promise, yet not a glib one. The psalmist envisions us meditating on the Psalms deeply enough that through them we may become "planted," securely established in wisdom and righteousness. It is indeed the case that for those who become so planted, everything yields some good fruit. Not that everything comes out the way they had hoped. Rather, the fruit of their action is that "God knows [their] way" (1: 6); in everything they do, they are still recognizable to the God who made them. A beautiful contemporary prayer of thanksgiving written by Charles Price expresses just such a complex understanding of prosperity: "We thank you also for those disappointments and failures that lead us to acknowledge our dependence on you alone."[1]

The Psalms have long been seen as uniquely valuable for those who seek to prosper thus.

All Scripture of ours...is inspired by God and prof-itable for teaching, as it is written [2 Timothy 3:16]. But the Book of Psalms possesses a certain winning exactitude for those who are prayerful.[2]

So wrote Athanasius, the fourth-century bishop of Alexandria, in a letter to his spiritual directee Marcellinus—a letter that is in fact the earliest handbook on praying the Psalms. The phrase "winning exactitude" implies that there is something to aim at in prayer, a target to which we can hope to come close, maybe even hit dead on. But the other side of that implication is the reality that it is possible to pray and not hit anything at all; sheer expenditure of energy does not count. The Psalms may help us to improve our aim when we pray, for they serve as a corrective to two common weaknesses, even dangers, in the life of prayer.

First, the Psalms are a corrective to idiosyncrasy in prayer. The Psalter is ancient Israel's book of *common* prayer. Praying these words, we are self-consciously taking our place among generations of faithful Israelites, Jews, and Christians. As Martin Luther says, the great value of the Psalter is that it relates not only the *works* of the "saints" (in the nontechnical sense) but also their *words*. The rest of scripture presents examples of the deeds of the saints—behavior that, Luther notes, it may be dangerous or impossible to imitate. But the Psalter is the most practical and accessible guide to the holy life:

> The Psalter holds you to the communion of the saints and away from the sects. For it teaches you in joy, fear, hope, and sorrow to think and speak as all the saints have thought and spoken.[3]

The Psalms give us words for all the moods in which we come before God: adoration, exultation, gratitude; but also rage, despair, fear—those feelings which, as "saints," we feel

12

required to deny. However, as we take the Psalms on our lips one by one, we eventually claim each of those experiences and feelings as our own, and thus we enter fully into the life of all those who call themselves Israel. What is distinctive about Israel's religious perception is this very knowledge that we are called into fully intimate relationship with the God who created the heavens and the earth, a relationship that is both probing and transformative. It begins with honest confession of our thoughts and feelings; yet the terms of the relationship are that we must always be willing to grow and change profoundly. So the Psalms honor our immediate personal experience, yet at the same time they keep us from becoming mired in it. This is not only because they are common prayer, but even more because, as we shall see, the Psalms are a dynamic form of prayer.

The Psalms guard us also against a second spiritual danger, what has been called "the primordial threat to humankind...namely, religion." "Religion" in the dangerous sense is a set of ideas *about* God, abstracted from an ongoing relationship *with* God—that is, religious notions that have been purified from all the ups and downs, the challenges to our self-satisfaction and certainty, that are part of any intimate relationship. Such pure religion can easily become stultifying to ourselves and threatening to others. This threat is manifested in the history of religious wars, and also in the personal histories of many who have grown up in "religious" environments. Because the Psalms are prayers, they force us to do more than engage in reasonable speculation about God. Using their words brings us into direct encounter: through them we find ourselves talking to the living God, sometimes in language we would never have imagined would come from our lips into God's ear.

Notes

1. "A Prayer of Thanksgiving," *The Book of Common Prayer* (New York: Church Hymnal Corporation, 1979), 836; hereafter BCP.

2. Athanasius, *The Life of Anthony and the Letter to Marcellinus,* trans. Robert Gregg (New York: Paulist Press, 1980), 101.

3. Preface to the Psalms, *Luther's Works*, ed. E. T. Bachmann and H. T. Lehmann (Philadelphia: Muhlenberg Press, 1960), 35:256.

13

Chapter Two

"WITH MY TEARS I MELT MY MATTRESS"

The Psalms of Lament

THERE IS A GREAT surprise in store for those who begin praying through the Psalms and discover many psalms that rarely, if ever, find their way into the Sunday service. The incomparable surprise gift in the Psalter is the psalms of lament. They dominate the first half of the Psalter (Psalms 1-72, see Psalm 72:20) known as "the prayers of David." These cries of anguish and rage would seem to violate all the rules for Christian prayer. First of all, the psalmists focus so much on themselves. Most of these laments start with "me": Look at me, God, listen to me. It is "I" and "me," my trouble and my salvation, all the way through. Moreover, these prayers are not polite. The psalmists accuse God of abandonment (22:2, 88:14), of murder (22:16), of falling asleep on the job (44:24). They try to bribe God (6:6; see the treatment on page 16). They tell God just to go away (39:13). Finally, and most offensively, the psalmists take an un-Christian attitude toward their enemies: they pray devoutly that terrible things will happen to them, even to little children (109:6-20, 137:9, 143:12).

Nonetheless, the sheer number of these laments forces us to take them seriously as a biblical model for prayer. They constitute the largest category of psalms in the Bible, outnumbering even the psalms of thanksgiving. Now this is a curious thing, because the Hebrew name for the Psalter is *Tehillîm,* "Praises." It is called the Book of Praises, yet it includes more laments than anything else. Pondering this contradiction might provide a good way to sharpen your aim in prayer. Here is a starting point for that meditation: When you lament in good faith, opening yourself to God honestly and fully—no matter what you have to say—then you are beginning to clear the way for praise. You are straining toward the time when God will turn your tears into laughter. When you lament, you are asking God to create the conditions in which it will become possible for you to offer praise—conditions, it turns out, that are mainly within your own heart.

The preponderance of laments in the Book of Praises is a fruitful contradiction from which we can learn much. But we live with a second discrepancy that should trouble us more than it does; namely, the contrast between the biblical models of prayer and our own contemporary practices in the church. It seems that ancient Israel believed that the kind of prayer in which we most need fluency is the loud groan, and they have bequeathed us a lot of material on which to practice. Therefore it is troubling that most Christians are almost completely unfamiliar with the lament psalms. Except on Ash Wednesday and Good Friday, these psalms almost never appear in worship services. Evidently modern Christian liturgists define the business of worship more narrowly than did ancient Israel, and as a result our lives as individual believers and as a church are impoverished. The shape of the

Psalter—the fact that the laments are brought to the fore—suggests that our own worship is deformed by our failure to bring the language of suffering into the sanctuary as an integral part of our weekly liturgy. The dimensions of our loss become clearer through looking carefully at Psalm 6, one of the lament psalms:

16

1   To the choirmaster, with instrumental music
      on the "eighth,"[1]
    a psalm for David.

2   LORD, do not in your wrath chastise me,
    and do not in your fury discipline me.

3   Be gracious to me, LORD, for I am languishing.
    Heal me LORD, for my bones are rattled.

4   And my being is very rattled.
    And you, LORD—how long?

5   Turn, LORD, deliver my being!
    Save me for the sake of your covenant loyalty!

6   For in death there is no remembrance of you.
    In Sheol, who gives thanks to you?

7   I am exhausted with my groaning.
    I make my bed swim every night;
    With my tears I melt my mattress.

8   My eye is worn out from vexation,
    grown old because of all my foes.

9   Get away from me, all you workers of iniquity!
    For the LORD has heard the sound of my weeping.

10 The LORD has heard my plea-for-grace;
     the LORD takes up my prayer.

11 They will be confounded and very rattled,
all my enemies;
they will turn and be confounded in an instant.

The thing to look for in a lament psalm is how it moves. 17
For almost invariably, the psalmist comes out in a different
place than she first entered into prayer; her view of the situation and of God shifts in the course of praying. The individual psalms were composed by many different poets, all of
them anonymous—although many were connected with the
royal court and the guilds of temple musicians. They were
genuinely creative poets, not hack writers plugging words
into fixed formulae. Nonetheless, the laments tend to follow
a fairly regular pattern of movement: beginning with *petition*
and *complaint* addressed to God, they move, however fitfully, in the direction of *praise*.

The first word in this psalm is the most important:
"LORD" (YHWH).[2] It is the most frequently repeated word in
the poem: eight times the psalmist names God as the focus
of hope and the source of help. This observation is crucial
for our understanding of what kind of poem this is. The fact
that God is addressed directly in the first line of this and
every other lament marks the beginning of a dialogue. The
psalmist is not just indulging in self-pity or "wishing
upwards,"[3] with no particular hope of satisfaction.

The center of gravity in the laments is located in the
psalmist's pleas to God and complaints about acute suffering
(6:2-8). My bones are rattled, my being is rattled...and you,
LORD—how long? How long are you going to stand by and
watch? The psalmist has to screw up his courage to pose that
thinly veiled accusation. We watch him wind up, first fend-
ing off God's anger (6:2), and then three times emphasizing
his own piteous condition (6:3-4a). Yet even with this cautious beginning, the whole prayer bespeaks a bold assumption: God cares that I am in pain and can be expected to do

something about it. That is a remarkable assumption when you think about it, which we hardly ever do—that the God who made heaven and earth should care that I am hurting. Yet it is the only thing that explains this strange style of biblical prayer, a style without parallel in the ancient world. In no other culture did people pray to the high god in language that was so strong, so forthright, even so rude: "Wake up, God! Why are you sleeping? We haven't forgotten you; why have you forgotten us?" (44:21, 24-25). Here the psalmist makes a more subtle appeal to God's "covenant loyalty" (6: 5), but still there is a discernible kick to it. The psalmist is saying, "We have a deal, LORD, and it's high time you made good on it!"

Next, veiled accusation turns to veiled threat: "In death there is no remembrance of you" (6:6). This is an appeal to God's enlightened self-interest; the psalmist is proffering the bargaining chip of praise. For as ancient Israel conceived it, the only thing God wants that humans have to offer is praise, and only the living can praise God. Our psalmist, like almost all the others, takes the standard Old Testament view that the dead are insentient, and Sheol is a place of silence.[4] From this she draws a crucial inference: If only the living can praise God, then my life is more than incidental to God's well-being. The divine reputation depends on my staying above ground.

My favorite expression of this deep Israelite conviction comes from Joshua at Ai. The Israelite army has just suffered its first defeat in the "conquest" of the Promised Land. Joshua, the new commander, in a mood comparable to that of our psalmist, addresses God along these lines: "They're making mincemeat out of us here on the field, God. And by the way... if the Canaanites cut off *our* name from the Land, what are you going to do about *your* big Name?" (Joshua 7:9). Call it covenant faith or call it *ḥutzpah*, Joshua is pointing to the fundamental article of biblical religion, namely, that God's life, God's glory, even God's well-being, are indissolubly linked with our lives. For Christians, the sublime expression of that indissoluble linkage between God's glory and frail human life is the incarnation of God in Jesus Christ. Correspondingly, in response to the question that Joshua poses, God gives the ultimate answer in the resurrection of Jesus Christ from the dead.

19

That divine answer becomes clearer if we phrase the question in less personal terms than does Joshua: "Is God's glory diminished, or extinguished, by human death?" Joshua and the psalmist would both answer: "Definitely! That is why God cannot let me die." And in a sense, all the heirs of biblical faith, Jews and Christians alike, have come to hold the same conviction, that ultimately God must triumph over human death. One of the many doctrinal points on which religious Jews and Christians agree is that God resurrects the dead. The doctrine of the resurrection may push far beyond what Joshua and the psalmist envisioned. Yet one might say that the seed of that doctrine lies in their belief that God can be coaxed and even coerced into saving their skin. Without the urgent expectation of those gutsy believers, I doubt that anyone would ever have come to that doctrinal position. So now we begin to see why the Psalms are so central to Christian faith. They push so hard at God, and, in the most personal terms, they push the envelope of our own limited faith. And sometimes—even over the course of centuries—they break into new realms of religious understanding.

Now here is a complaint that makes it worth God's time to listen to our prayer, especially if God is a blues fan:

I make my bed swim every night;
With my tears I melt my mattress. (6:7)

In addition to its directness, the most striking thing about the language of the lament psalms is the poets' use of metaphors. Poem after poem, line after line, listen for those vivid metaphors that tell you exactly how bad it feels: "Along my back the plowmen plowed" (129:3). What is the "it" that feels so bad? That we don't know. "All my bones are out of joint" (22:15) probably does not indicate an orthopedic problem. The psalmists habitually give few, if any, circumstantial details. Yet this metaphorical latitude, this combination of precision about the feeling and vagueness about the circumstances, makes these psalms available for use by any of us. Like the blues, anybody in pain can sing them—or anybody who has ever been in pain and wants to remember what it is like, in order to keep compassion alive. Listen to what the metaphors are telling us about how our neighbor feels: "I am like a skin bottle in the smoke" (119:83)—I am dry, cracked, leaky, and therefore disposable. How many people do we know or see who feel that way: jobless youths in the inner city, the frail elderly, executives who have been laid off, homemakers for whom life was emptied of its old meaning when children left home, or when a spouse died or departed? So let the metaphors of the lament psalms help you express your grief. And when you are not yourself in grief, let them instruct your compassion.

At the end of Psalm 6, as generally in the laments, there is a sudden shift in mood. Almost without exception, the lament psalms end with a clear expectation of deliverance. Often the psalmist looks forward to throwing a praise party at the temple to make God's "big Name" even bigger: "I shall croon the Name of the LORD Most High" (7:18). Yet strangely (from our ordinary perspective), the psalmist is planning the party while still surrounded by enemies: "Get away from me, all you workers of iniquity!" (6:9). Here is a remarkable thing: the lament psalms regularly trace a movement from complaint to confidence in God, from desperate petition to anticipatory praise. Yet they make that move *without ever telling us that the external situation has changed for the better.* In this example, workers of iniquity are evidently as threatening as ever. What has changed is the psalmist's experience of suffering, and perhaps that has changed only because she has dared to break the isolation of silence and knows that God has heard.

21

The fact that the Psalms never clearly report a change in external circumstances is one mark of the Bible's persistent realism. Prayer is not always answered in the terms we expect and long for; the answer may be given in a way that is not even perceptible to someone looking at the situation from the outside. God answered intense prayers for my friend Marty's healing as she was dying from a brain tumor. During the fifteen months following the operation that confirmed her diagnosis, she was steadily and at last fully healed from a lifelong sickness of sadness. It was a time of growing joy and freedom, a period punctuated by laughter as well as tears, as Marty gradually shed the crippling anxiety she had known for a lifetime. She died on Holy Saturday, and she died confident that she had been delivered.

One further mark of the realism of the Psalter is the fact that it includes two psalms—Psalms 39 and 88—that make no turn toward praise. The very existence of these exceptional psalms is important, for it suggests that unresolved despair is itself one legitimate, though tragic, aspect of our life with God. Crying out to God, screaming at God in the darkness—like Job, refusing false comfort yet still being unable to rise and embrace hope—there is room for that also in the life of faithful prayer. In the final scene of the film *Sophie's Choice*, a man travels to claim and bury the bodies of two friends, a Holocaust survivor and her lover who died as suicides, ultimately unable to bear the burden of memory.

On the bus ride he meets an older African-American woman, who lines out for him the words of Psalm 88, which concludes thus:

22

> You [God] have removed from me lover
>   and companion.
> My intimates are...darkness!

The woman on the bus had inherited some of the wisdom of the psalmists, who understood that sometimes the only act of faith that is possible—for those who suffer and those who minister to them—is to name our desolation before God, and to implicate God in our suffering.[5]

Notes

1. The meaning of this notation is not known—perhaps an eight-stringed instrument, or the eighth stage of a ritual?

2. By biblical and Jewish tradition, the name of God (YHWH) is too sacred to be pronounced. The Tetragrammeton ("Four Letters") is commonly rendered into English as LORD.

3. The phrase comes from Eugene Peterson, *Answering God: The Psalms as Tools for Prayer* (San Francisco: Harper & Row, 1989), 15.

4. The poet of Psalm 22 is an important exception. It is not coincidence that this psalm, which envisions the dead worshipping God (v. 30), was a model for the early church in recounting the story of Jesus' death and resurrection.

5. Chapter ten, on the book of Job, further develops this theme.

CHAPTER THREE

BUT SURELY NOT THOSE!

The Cursing Psalms

"SURELY YOU DO NOT mean to say that any Christian should pray those psalms! It is because of words like those that the Old Testament should be burned and the ashes cast into the sea!" The reaction was strongly worded, but probably others shared at least the first part of the sentiment. I had just finished a defense of the cursing psalms in a teaching session at my own parish, where people were willing to be frank. Yes, I do mean to say that Christians should pray these offensive psalms that call down God's wrath upon our enemies. Or better, we should know that these psalms are available and even appropriate for Christian prayer, and sometimes they are necessary. But like many good tools, they must be used responsibly, or they become dangerous to ourselves and to others.

Psalm 109 is the most extended of these cursing psalms. The poem begins like many laments, with a complaint about enemies:

> God of my praise, do not be deaf!
> For the mouth of the wicked
> and the mouth of deceit have opened against me.
> (109:1-2)

The special poignancy of the cursing psalms stems from the fact that the enemies are not faceless. They are people well known to the psalmist, even dear friends, from whom he has every reason to expect love in return for his own:

> Words of hatred surround me.
> They make war against me for no reason!
> In exchange for my love, they oppose me—
> yet I am all prayer! (109:3-4)

The psalmist is, indeed, "all prayer." Here is how he prays now for his erstwhile friend:

> Set over *him* a wicked man;
> let an opponent stand at his right hand.
> When he is judged, let him come out guilty;
> and let his prayer miss its target.[1]
> May his days be few;
> let another take his possessions.
> May his children be orphans,
> and his wife a widow.
> May his children wander about and beg,
> going in search away from their hovels. (109:6-10)

You have not heard these words in church. Sunday lectionaries omit psalms like this altogether, or they include them in highly expurgated form. But by clapping our hand over the psalmist's mouth in that way, we lose something the Bible intends us to have. By refusing to listen to that anger and even take it on our lips, we lose an opportunity to bring our own anger into the context of our relationship with God. The cursing psalms are in fact a crucial resource for our spiritual growth, indispensable if we are to come before God with rigorous honesty. They are necessary not only for our individual spiritual health but also for maintaining or restoring the health of the church. For these psalms reckon directly with a feature of church life which is almost never acknowledged: the phenomenon of betrayal within the faith community. Once, attending a eucharistic service at a theological college that prepared students for mission work, we gathered around the altar and chanted Taizé-style:

We are here at the table of the Lord.
We are not alone.
We are here with our enemies.

Is there any congregation that meets regularly where that chant could not honestly and helpfully be used? Maybe it draws inspiration from the most poignant of the cursing psalms:

It is not an enemy who reviles me;
that I could bear.
It is not my opponent who vaunts himself
    against me;
I could hide from him.
But you, someone just like me,
my companion and my intimate;
we shared sweet fellowship
in the house of God,
we walked in the crowd. (55:13-15)

The cursing psalms help us to hold our anger in good faith. Sadly, most of us feel about our enemies more like the psalmist does than like Jesus did. We must pray to be healed from our hardness of heart, but healing will not come through a cover-up. Healing for ourselves and even for our enemies requires that we acknowledge our bitter feelings and yet not yield to their tyranny. Rather we must offer them, along with our more attractive gifts, for God's work of transformation. In several ways, the cursing psalms give us strong practical guidance in making that offering of anger.

First, *they give us words for our anger* when we are too stunned by its enormity to find our own. As a young seminarian, I had a bitter experience of betrayal by a close friend within the community—a classic case for use of the cursing psalms, although I did not know that. But my pastoral theology professor saw my need, and he gave me a list of psalm numbers with the advice: "Go into the chapel when no one else is around and shout these at the top of your lungs." It was the most helpful advice anyone gave me at the time—especially the part about shouting. That the psalms provided a vent for my anger is obvious. Less obvious, and much more important, they helped me move beyond blind rage. After a few days and nights, my own loud rantings began to sound a little different to my ears. Angry as I still was, I could hear in them a faint note of self-righteousness, even pettiness. "Your decrees are my counselors," the psalmist says (119:24). Like a wise friend, these psalms were giving me company in my anger and at the same time instructing me through my self-consciousness. For the cursing psalms confront us with one of our most persistent idolatries, to which neither Israel nor the church has ever been immune: the belief that God has as little use for our enemies as we do, the desire to reduce God to an extension of our own embattled and wounded egos.

Second, because these psalms come to us as divinely given "counselors," we can trust their teaching that *vengeful anger is one mode of access to God.* "O God of my praise" (109:1), the psalmist begins. The cry for vengeance is not self-expression but prayer, based on what we know to be true: God is manifest in judgment as well as in mercy. The God who created us for life together (Genesis 2:18) is, like us, outraged by those who violate trust and rupture community. The cursing psalms obliquely affirm that every believer has a share in the prophetic task of naming and renouncing evil, including evil within the community of faith, including evil that is directed against ourselves. There is nothing pre-Christian about that. Our baptismal vows require us to make the same affirmation, when the candidate (or her parents) responds in the affirmative to the question: "Do you renounce the evil powers of this world which corrupt and destroy the creatures of God?" (BCP 302).

The third and most important direction these psalms offer is that *the cry for vengeance invariably takes the form of an appeal for God to act.*

> Help me, O LORD my God;
> deliver me according to your covenant loyalty
> that they may know that this hand of yours—
> you yourself, O LORD, have done it. (109:26-27)

No personal vendetta is authorized, no pouring sugar in the gas tank, no picking up a gun or hiring one. On the contrary, the validity of any punishing action that may occur depends entirely on its being God's action, not ours. And readers of the Bible recognize that this is in fact a severely limiting condition. For God's action is free, directed not only to our healing but to the healing of the whole moral order. Through these psalms we demand that our enemies be driven into God's hands. But who can say what will happen to them there? For God is manifest in judgment of our enemies but also, alas, in mercy toward them. Thus these vengeful psalms have a relationship with other forms of prayer for our enemies. I once heard someone in the course of praying turn a cursing psalm into intercessory prayer for the one who had hurt her. That is the prerogative of the one praying. Not everyone can take that step, and no one should take it prematurely. "There is a time to embrace, and a time to refrain from embracing" (Ecclesiastes 3:5). Yet even while we are still in our anger, the cursing psalms are the vehicle whereby we yield to God our own claim to vengeance, and that is the crucial first step to the healing of the entire community.

All that I have said applies to praying the cursing psalms when we are angry. But do they have any use when we are not? It is worth noting that they appear in set lectionaries for daily usage, even in unexpurgated form. Now, suppose you run across one of these psalms when you are blessedly free of the feelings they articulate. Is there any prayer opportunity for you then? The ancient rabbis said of scripture: "Turn it and turn it, for everything is in it." If you have the courage (and it will take some), try turning the psalm a full 180 degrees, until it is directed at yourself, and ask: Is there anyone in the community of God's people who might want to say this to God about me—or maybe, about us?

Here is one of several ways I could answer that question for myself: I am materially privileged beyond most people who are alive at this time, who have previously lived on the earth, or who will live in future generations. By social location, income, and personal habit, I am an active participant in a rapacious industrial economy, regularly consuming far more than I need of the world's goods. I have largely failed to moderate my lifestyle in accordance with what I can reasonably expect will be the needs of my great-grandchildren's generation, to say nothing of the present needs of those living today in the Two-Thirds World. Yes, there are those who might cry out to God this night or fifty years hence:

> Let [her] memory be cut off from the earth,
> because [she] did not remember to act in
>   covenant faith
> but hounded a person poor and needy,

crushed in heart, even to death. . . .
But you, O LORD, act with me as befits your Name.
Because your covenant faithfulness is good,
   deliver me.
For I am poor and needy,
and my heart is pierced within me.

(109:16, 21-22)

29

God give me courage to hear that prayer and act upon what
I have heard.

Notes

1. The line may be translated "Let his prayer become sin." My
translation reflects the fact that the Hebrew word for "sin" literally
means "missing a target." See Athanasius's comment, cited on page
11, about the "winning exactitude" of the Psalms.

CHAPTER FOUR

"LAMENTING INTO DANCING"

The Psalms of Praise

ISRAEL KNOWS ITSELF as a people that has been put on the planet—and much more than that, preserved alive and kept in faith against incredible odds—for the express purpose of praising God. So even when Israel is lamenting, it is always looking for opportunities to praise. The lament psalms are prayers of anguish yearning to be transformed into praise. The psalmists typically end their poems imagining their own prayer dramatically changed:

> And as for me, I will walk in my integrity—
> redeem me and be gracious to me!
> My foot stands on level ground.
> In gatherings-of-the-faithful I will praise the LORD.
>   (26:11-12)

So lament is always hoping to grow into praise; when it does, it does not forget where it came from. If we look carefully at the psalms of praise (broadly speaking, almost any psalm that is not a lament), then we will see that some grievous situation now past is always in the background. Or perhaps the act of giving praise is itself a way of putting anxiety or grief behind us. The verbs in the following psalm leave the time sequence unclear; it is by no means certain that danger is wholly past.[1]

> I exalt you, O LORD, for you pulled me up;
> and you did not let my enemy rejoice over me.
> O LORD, I cried out to you
> and you healed me....
> To you, O LORD, I call out;
> and to my LORD I make supplication.
> "What is the profit in my blood, in my going down
>   to the Pit?
> Does dust praise you? Does it tell out your
>   faithfulness?
> Hear, O LORD, and be gracious to me.
> LORD, be my helper!"
> You have turned my lamenting into dancing for me.
> You have removed my sackcloth and girded me
>   with joy,
> that [my] whole being might hymn you and never
>   be silent.
> O LORD my God, forever I will give you thanks!
>   (30:2-3, 9-13)

This psalm is the companion piece to Psalm 6. In that lament we heard the psalmist twisting the divine arm with a promise of praise. Evidently, it worked! When we view the psalms of praise against the background of recent or even ongoing distress, they no longer seem boring or routine. (I am forced to conclude that most preachers do see them as boring; for we read psalms of praise nearly every Sunday morning, yet only a few times in my life have I heard one explored in a sermon.) On the contrary, psalms of praise, no less than laments, are sung in full awareness of the unrelenting difficulty of human life. "In the midst of life, we are in death."[2] Israel is not a sanguine people; even their joyful prayers are never laid back, never naive. "Everything works for the best in this best of all possible worlds": Pangloss (in Voltaire's *Candide*) is certainly no Israelite. The psalmists read reality in a very different way. They are always aware that survival in this difficult world depends entirely on the slender thread of prayer and covenant faithfulness that binds us to God.

In Psalm 30, the psalmist praises God for a specific act of deliverance, although in accordance with the generalizing nature of the psalms, it is unspecified here. But sometimes the psalmist praises God just for being God, as in Psalm 33:

1 Sing joyfully, you righteous, to the LORD;
   to the straightforward, praise is becoming.

2 Give thanks to the LORD on the lyre;
   with ten stringed harp, hymn him!

3 Sing to him a new song;
   perform a skillful melody with ringing shouts.

4 For the word of the LORD is straightforward,
   and all his doing is with faithfulness.

5 A lover of righteousness and justice,
   the LORD's covenant love fills the earth.

6 With the word of the LORD, the heavens were made,
   and with the breath of his mouth, all their host.

7 He gathers up as in a heap the waters of the sea,
   setting in storehouses the deeps.

8 Let all the earth stand in fear of the LORD;
   let all the world's inhabitants be in awe of him.

9 For he spoke, and it was.
He commanded, and it stood.

10 The LORD breaks the counsel of nations;
he frustrates the plans of peoples.

33

11 The counsel of the LORD stands forever,
the thoughts of his heart to generation after
generation.

12 Privileged is the nation whose God is the LORD;
the people he has chosen for his own inheritance.

13 From the heavens the LORD looked;
he saw all the human creatures.

14 From his dwelling place he peered down
toward all the earth-dwellers—

15 the One who entirely fashions their heart,
who comprehends all their doings.

16 There is no king who is victorious by a great force;
a hero is not delivered by great strength.

17 A lie! the horse for victory—
even by its great force, it does not save.

18 See, the eye of the LORD is on those who fear him;
on those who are hoping for his covenant love

19 to deliver their being from death
and to keep them alive in famine.

20 Our very being waits for the LORD.
He is our help and our shield;

21 for in him our heart rejoices,
for in his holy Name we trust.

22 Let your covenant love, LORD, be upon us,
even as we hope in you.

"To the straightforward, praise is becoming" (53:1)—this
might be the core insight from which all the psalms of praise
proceed. Praise is more than something we do for God.
Although the psalmists are not wholly above using praise as
a bargaining chip,[3] they would encourage us to see the bigger picture. The truth is that praise does more for *us* than it
does for God. (It is time for Christians to get over the adolescent idea that the main reason to go to church is so that
God won't be disappointed.) Praise looks good on the
straightforward, on those who aspire to look at the world
realistically, unsentimentally—that is, those who aspire *not*
to view the world through the distorting lens of their own
fantastic desires. In other words, praise suits those who want
to see the world as it really is.

This is a crucial insight about the essential function of
praise. Praising God is not concocted flattery, but the most
earnest human business we can undertake. Ultimately, it is
for the sake of the world: we praise God in order to see the
world as God does. So, setting aside our own groundless fan-
tasies, the alternative viewing lens that this psalm offers is
"the word of the LORD." God's word is itself "straightforward" (33:4), just as *we* may hope to be. In our parlance, "the
word of the LORD" usually designates the Bible itself. But the
psalmist means something more general than that, namely,
God's expressed will for the world. It is expressed verbally
through the traditions of prophets, priests, and scribes, but
also in acts of "righteousness and justice" (33:5). That is, all
actions that serve to maintain the rights of the weak and
secure the well-being of every creature God has made—all
these are God's "word" to us, articulating the Creator's good
intentions for the creatures. These myriad actions, both
divine and human, are how the earth becomes full of God's

"covenant love" (Hebrew *ḥesed*,[4] 33:5), that quality which is the hallmark of the divine personality. One English word does not adequately convey the full sense of this most fundamental "word" of Israel's God, a word that expresses unswerving loyalty to the covenant partner, compassion extended to someone in need, even nurturing love of an affectionate kind.[5] Most often, *ḥesed* is invoked in the context of God's covenant with Israel.[6] But the psalmist understands that God's covenantal loyalty has the broadest possible scope. The very first demonstration of God's *ḥesed* was the ordering of the cosmos (33:6-7); this in turn should remind us that God made the first covenant not with Israel, not even with humankind alone, but with the earth itself (Genesis 9:13; compare 9:11).

The picture of God's *ḥesed* filling the earth is a saving word to the "straightforward" in this generation. The psalms of praise are among the most powerful bearers of ecological vision in the Bible, because they delineate in such beautiful detail the work of the Creator (for example, Psalms 29, 65, 104). If we pray them with an open heart, they expand our understanding of this "righteousness and justice" that God so loves beyond our immediate social sphere. As the biblically minded theologian Thomas Aquinas taught, justice is the primary duty that the human creature owes to every other creature, and we owe it precisely as one creature to another. In the early twenty-first century, we are only now coming to see that the Bible's expansive view of covenantal justice is in fact essential for our survival. In order to understand fully the demands of justice in our present situation, we need to be like legal experts, reviewing the history pertinent to the case. And this psalm reminds us that the relevant history goes back to the first chapter of the Bible, to the first divine word expressing God's will for the world: "He spoke, and it was" (33:9).

36

The chief contrast in this psalm is between those who do and those who do not recognize God's "counsel," the divine will expressed in creation and in scripture, as determinative for their lives (33:10-12). The latter, quite simply, become the casualties of history (33:16-17). But the former are "privileged" (33:12). This is the same Hebrew word (*'ashrê*) that lies behind Jesus' Beatitudes: "Privileged are the poor in spirit, for theirs is the kingdom of heaven" (Matthew 5:3). Maybe Jesus even had our psalm in mind. Certainly it offers one fair definition of "the poor in spirit": those people, even those nations (our psalmist has a big vision), who are able to see beyond their own inevitably delusive "counsel" (33:10). In other words, they live under the immediate sovereignty of God and do not comfort themselves with false sources of security: kings and their horses (33:16-17). In both Psalm 33 and the Beatitudes, God's sovereignty ("the kingdom of heaven") is the standard by which "righteousness and justice" will be judged.

See how the psalmist encourages us to take the seeming risk of choosing that sovereign counsel over all earthly forms of security. It would be more accurate to say that our choice is simply a matter of accepting God's prior choice: "Privileged is ... the people he has chosen for his own inheritance" (33:12). The psalm pictures God's exquisite interest in the inhabitants and the events of this world (33:13-15). The great Creator leaning forward to peer through the cloud floor, eager to see all that happens among "the earth-dwellers"—how different this image is from ancient pagan notions of deity. As both Mesopotamian and Greek myths represent it, the tragedy of human existence is the capriciousness of the universe. There is a perpetual anxiety that attends paganism, first of all because the gods are more interested in power-brokering among themselves than in showing mercy to humanity. (Recall that the progress of the

Trojan War reflects the ebb and flow of domestic quarrels among gods.) Moreover, even if the god to whom you are praying is on your side, you can never be sure *that* god is in charge of *this* situation. But Psalm 33 emphasizes in the strongest terms both God's total sovereignty over every aspect of creation (33:6-8, 15) and also the bond that is being actively sustained between God and ourselves every day. The strength of this bond depends on the good faith of both parties, evidenced on the one side by God's patient concern for "those who are hoping for his covenant love" (33:18), and on the other, by our patient confidence in God: "Our very being waits for the LORD" (33:20).

So, like the laments, this psalm of praise ends with anticipation. God's praise is sung in the middle of history, by those who are still looking for God's covenant love to be fully manifest in every aspect of their lives (33:22). The final lines bespeak confidence in God (33:21), but that does not wholly dissolve the tension that is present to some degree, at least, in all prayer. For people who pray are people living in hope. Biblical tradition associates prayer with hope more consistently than with satisfaction. Standing firmly in this tradition, the apostle Paul instructs the gentile Christians in Rome: "Rejoice in hope, be patient in suffering, persevere in prayer" (Romans 12:12). Maybe it would be better to say that Paul is *suspended* firmly in this tradition of the hopeful. From a biblical perspective, hope may be best imaged as a line suspended between past experience of God's reliability and a future that is still open, a line stretched taut between the reliability and the freedom of Israel's God. That accounts for the note of keen anticipation so characteristic of the Psalms.

Yet even as Israel waits upon God, the psalmist urges the righteous to sing joyfully (33:1). And in that call to rejoice lies a profound understanding of worship. We cannot defer

37

praising God until we are fully satisfied with our situation. The basic dynamic of praise is not that God gives us something and we say, "Thanks," out of surfeited hearts. Instead, through praise we discover how much we have in fact *already* been given. Through the language of faithful worship, we come to see the world as it really is: the work of God's hand, the object of God's endlessly patient love. What is more, through praise we come to a new perception of our own situation. We do not have to strive continually to secure a place for ourselves. That place has been provided. There is a basic givenness of reality on which we can rely: "all [God's] doing is with faithfulness" (33:4). In resting upon that reliability, in accepting the remarkable givenness of our place in this world, we find our happiness. Thus, we recognize ourselves as a people blessed by the very fact of being in covenant relationship with this God (33:12). That it what it means for us, as Christians, to claim an identity with the people Israel.

It is probable that the area of ancient Israel's greatest creativity was the praise of God. Other cultures were magnificently skilled in the fine arts or the practical arts, in architecture or astronomy, sculpture or ivory work, embalming or warfare. Some of that ancient work remains unsurpassed to this day. What Israelites did best was praise God, and they knew it: "Every day I will bless you, and praise your Name for ever and ever" (145:2). That tradition is maintained to this day, as Jews and Christians continue to pray the Psalms. Yet Christians are generally unaware that there is another important source for keeping the vitality of that tradition alive: the large collection of post-biblical blessings preserved in the Jewish prayer book.[7] Some familiarity with these can help us be inventive in our praise.

Many Christians are familiar with the Jewish blessings over bread and wine that are the basis of our eucharistic prayers: "Blessed are you, O LORD, King of the Universe, who

brings forth bread from the earth"; and "Blessed are you, O
LORD, King of the Universe, who creates the fruit of the vine."
There are dozens of other Jewish blessings, very specific
praises to be said when you eat eggs, when you see a falling
star or a beautiful tree, when you meet a good teacher, when
you hear good news or bad news. Most of these, like the
blessings over bread and wine, are just one line long. They
can be prayed on the spur of the moment, to capture our
gratitude and offer it to God, in no more time than it takes
to mutter the involuntary expressions of irritation that come
to most of us so easily.

My personal favorite among the Jewish blessings is a little
longer. It is intended to serve as the first major blessing of the
day and is included in public prayer at the early morning
prayer service. From an outsider's perspective this is remarkable, for the worshipers praise God that they have been able
to accomplish their toilet:

> Blessed are you, O LORD, King of the Universe, who
> formed humankind with wisdom, and created in
> them many orifices and passages. It is revealed and
> known before your throne of glory, that if one of them
> were open [that should be shut], or one of them were
> shut [that should be open], then it would be impossi-
> ble to exist and to stand before you. Blessed are you, O
> LORD, Healer of all flesh, who does wondrously.

No prayer could better fulfill the psalmist's thrilled vow of
praise:

> I will give thanks to you on account that I am
>   fearfully and wonderfully made.
> Wondrous are your works, and I know that well, in
>   the core of my being. (139:14)

39

Yet this homely praise sounds to us odd and embarrassing. (It should be acknowledged that mainstream American Protestants are easily embarrassed by praise. On any Sunday, you can bank on the fact that the prayers for healing and comfort will be lengthier than the thanksgivings.) However, from a biblical perspective what needs to be explained is not why the psalmists or contemporary orthodox Jews consider the perfectly ordinary worthy of celebration. The strange thing is that *we* do not more often think to give thanks for those daily miracles of "creation, preservation, and all the blessings of this life" (BCP 101)—starting with the fact that we awakened this morning in our right minds, that we can remember to give thanks at all. Such minutely specific blessings may be the best way for us to learn how to pray as we ought, for they aim at the basic purpose of all praise: to sanctify the world, to name it as holy. Saying those myriad tiny prayers is like seeing our world and our own life as a crystal, holding it up and letting light fall on its different facets. They remind us that nothing, nothing at all may be taken for granted. Everything we see and use and are is an expression of God's creative concern, and therefore an occasion for us to say, "Thanks."

Notes

1. "Imperfect" verb forms such as those in verse 9 normally convey ongoing action. Accordingly, I translate them in the present tense; perhaps the petition for help is still active.

2. This is the opening line of an anthem sung in the Episcopal burial office (BCP 484).

3. See the treatments of Psalms 6 and 30, pp. 16-17 and 31.

4. This sound (ḥ) is the guttural "h" as in the final sound of "Bach."

5. For example, Ruth demonstrates *ḥesed* toward both her mother-in-law Naomi and her future husband Boaz (Ruth 3:10).

6. For example, Psalm 98:3. One might assume that the covenant with Israel is the background in Psalm 6:5, page 16.

7. *The Standard Prayer Book* (New York: Bloch Publishing Company, 1915), 4.

PART TWO

THE COST OF LOVE

THESE CHAPTERS SHOW us something of how God got involved with one special family (Abraham's) and one people, and through them, with all humanity. Like any long-term intimate relationship, that involvement proves to be very costly on both sides. I highlight two moments in the recorded history of the relationship when, if we read sensitively, we can feel something of the cost: when God calls Abraham to take his son up on a mountaintop and offer him as a sacrifice, and when God calls to Moses out of a burning bush. Israel knows that being involved with God is costly. It demands everything from us, as these stories suggest. Yet it also gives us something rare and precious beyond measure. In the Song of Songs, we see the keenest celebration of the gift of intimacy between God and Israel, and an invitation to us to share in it.

CHAPTER FIVE

"I'VE GOT TO TURN ASIDE"

The Burning Bush

> And Moses said, "I've got to turn aside so I may see this great sight: why is the bush not burnt up?" (Exodus 3:3)[1]

THE BUSH THAT BURNS with fire and is not consumed—this is perhaps in all of scripture the most arresting image of God's holiness palpable on earth. "Take your sandals off your feet, for the place where you are standing, it's holy ground" (3:5)—not only a place where God is heard speaking, but the place where God comes down, all the way down to the ground: "I have come down to deliver [my people] from the hand of Egypt and to bring them up from that land" (3:8). The essence of the gospel is heard already from the burning bush: God has come down to holy ground to deliver us and to bring us up to a land of promise.

So I suppose it was inevitable that the early Greek theologians, with their wonderful associative imaginations, would see the link between the burning bush and the incarnation.

Gregory of Nyssa saw it first, in the fourth century, in his treatise *On the Birth of Christ,* and then later the iconographic tradition picked it up: the icon of Mary Mother of God as the burning bush hangs at St. Catherine's monastery at Mt. Sinai. Mary, who conceived by the Holy Spirit, yet remained a virgin; Mary, who carried God in her belly and later in her arms, yet did not dissolve to ash—she is herself the bush that burns perpetually, yet is not consumed.

That image of Mary, ancient and still fresh, may serve to refresh our reading of Moses' story, which suffers somewhat from over-familiarity. Mary and Moses have this in common: in the history of the world, they are the two people who have known God most intimately, known God in ways that mortal flesh ordinarily could not tolerate without burning to a cinder. The Israelites understood that trespassing on holy ground would bring instant death. The high priest took his life in his hands when he entered the Holy of Holies one day each year, and even he entered the holy place enveloped in smoke, for who could see God and live? Yet God spoke to Moses "face to face, as one speaks to a friend" (Exodus 33:11)—in one place, scripture says "mouth-to-mouth" (Numbers 12:8).

That is intimate. If God has a best friend (and why not?), then surely it is Moses. At moments we see Moses sass God, when things are not going well in the wilderness. And not only does he get away with it, but God accommodates his complaints and makes in-course corrections. God does not take a human being so fully into the divine confidence—you might say, God does not depend on a human being so fully—until Mary conceives by the Holy Spirit. These are the two more-or-less ordinary people in the history of the world with whom, it seems, God has felt most fully at home. Moses and Mary are the ones who made most room in their lives and therefore in our world for God's dramatically new work of deliverance. Knowingly and willingly, they welcomed God as God is, utterly demanding and utterly loving. That is why God could come so close, "mouth-to-mouth."

Thinking about Moses in conjunction with Mary helps us to focus on what is happening in this third chapter of Exodus. For here, in the first direct encounter between God and Moses, we see the beginning of an intimacy. Remember, we know very little about the grown man Moses at this point, so the way the biblical narrator presents him is important. Generally, the Bible reports only the essentials of the action—what someone says or does—and we infer the rest. In this account, these are the essentials: the angel, or God, appears to Moses in fire in the midst of the bush, and Moses turns aside to see. But there is something unusual about the way the narrator tells this story. For a moment, we get to hear what Moses is thinking. For an instant, we are inside Moses' head, as he decides to turn away from his father-in-law's flock and leave them behind: "I've got to turn aside so I may see this great sight: why is the bush not burnt up?" Moreover (and this is even more rare), we are given an indication of how God thinks: "*And when the LORD saw that he had turned aside,* God called to him from inside the bush, and he said, 'Moses, Moses!'" (3:4). Evidently it is Moses' conscious resolve—"I've got to turn aside"—to turn away from the task at hand and investigate "this great sight" that prompts God to speak to him for the first time.

Now what could God find compelling in this? It may be that God recognizes something characteristic of Moses here. For we have already seen Moses "turn aside," step out of line for something that turned out to be one of the things of God: the time when he killed an Egyptian for beating a Hebrew slave and fled for his life from his own grandfather Pharaoh into the Arabian desert (2:11-15). The Prince of Egypt there became a Midianite shepherd—until this

47

moment, when he "turns aside" and leaves the flock behind. Moses is like a locomotive who jumps the track: he will never get back on. Oh, he will return to Pharaoh's court, but not as the prodigal come home. Rather, he will come back as leader of the opposition who exposes Pharaoh's deadly self-idolatry. Moses will once again lead a flock through the wilderness, but from this moment on, he is done with sheep. Once he turns aside for the things of God—resolved, yet not knowing very well what he is doing—Moses never gets back on the old track.

If, as I suppose, God is drawn to Moses because of his capacity to be derailed for the sake of the things of God, then this also reveals something to us about God. Here I think we are close to the heart of this first revelation at Horeb (Sinai). At Sinai, God is revealed as a deity who jumps the track, a God who gets derailed for the sake of the things of humanity, for the sake of the people Israel. That revelation to Israel is a completely new way of seeing God. In the ancient pagan imagination, the high gods, the really big players, were ensconced in some heavenly realm where they—well, acted like gods. They squabbled and had love affairs among themselves; they feasted and accepted sacrifices from human beings. They might be propitiated or bribed to push events one way or the other on earth, but theirs was a very limited engagement with humanity. The drastically new thing that happened at Sinai is that the Creator of heaven and earth entered into *unlimited* engagement with the people Israel. Listen again:

> I have truly seen the affliction of my people who are in Egypt; their outcry I have heard, because of their oppressors; yes, I know their pain; and *I have come down* to deliver them from the hand of Egypt. (3:7-8)

"I have seen and I have heard and I have come down"—
in effect, God is saying, "I've got to turn aside. I know this
people's pain, and I cannot go on with business as usual." Do
you see? God, too, is like a locomotive who jumps the track
at Sinai, and really never gets back on. The way gods used to
be—distant figures, not touched in any essential way by
human pain—that path is closed forever to the God who
calls to Moses out of the burning bush.

49

If this is a true reading of the third chapter of Exodus,
then Gregory of Nyssa rightly saw that the burning bush and
the God-bearing body of Mary are ultimately one revelation
of God, separated only in time. For the gospel affirms that in
the fullness of time, the God of Israel, once again moved
beyond all reason by love and by pain, came down to deliver
not Israel only, but the whole world. The flame that burned
in the bush at Sinai is the same light to which Mary gave
birth. It burns yet and, for all our darkness, is not extinguished. We are in Epiphany, the season of light. Come then,
"take your sandals off your feet, for the place where you are
standing, it's holy ground."

Notes

1. This chapter has been adapted from a sermon for Epiphany.

CHAPTER SIX

"TAKE YOUR SON"

The Binding of Isaac

> And it happened, after these things, that God tested
> Abraham. And he said to him, "Abraham." And he said
> to him, "Here I am." And he said, "Take your son, your
> only one, whom you love, Isaac, and get you going to
> the land of the Moriah, and offer him up there as a
> burnt offering on one of the mountains which I shall
> indicate to you." (Genesis 22:1-2)

ABRAHAM AND HIS GOD are appalling. If this is a test,
then it would seem that both have failed miserably, both the
One who devised the test and the one who submitted to it.
What kind of God commands a father to sacrifice his only
son, lets him go through every agonized motion, and then
halts the action just as the knife has reached the top of its arc,
at the very moment of descent into the boy's throat? What
kind of father accepts the ostensible terms of this loyalty test?
"No, under no circumstances! Get thee behind me,
Satan!"—isn't *that* the right answer to this particular
demand from the realm of superhuman powers?

Our natural, instinctive response to this story is to reject it. Surely, it is a foreign element that has somehow been sneaked into our biblical tradition. It is not just pre-Christian but sub-Christian, antithetical to everything we know to be true about God the Father of Jesus Christ. I can only remember hearing one preacher take on this story directly, and his battle cry was, "I'm glad I don't worship the God of Abraham!" Shortly thereafter he moved from pulpit to altar and proceeded to contradict himself by reciting a eucharistic prayer which affirmed that we do, in fact, worship Abraham's (and Isaac's) God—or at least, we mean to.

A more sophisticated way to get rid of what is objectionable is to take an historical approach to the story. For a century now, theological students have grown up on the following "discovery" of historical criticism: this story marks a key juncture in the religious and ethical development of Israel—the point at which Israel rejected the archaic (and archaeologically well attested) pagan practice of burning babies to placate the deity. After all, Isaac was not slaughtered, but released at the divine command. This approach would then seem ideal for showing why the story of the Binding of Isaac[1] is in the Bible after all: Israel celebrates the breakthrough to "ethical religion" by connecting it to Abraham, its most illustrious ancestor. According to this view, Genesis 22 foreshadows the ringing prophetic statement:

With what shall I come before the LORD,
and bow low before God on high?
Will the LORD be pleased with thousands of rams,
with ten thousand torrents of oil?
Shall I give my first-born son for my transgression,
the fruit of my belly for the sin of my being?
He has told you, humanity, what is good,
And what the LORD demands from you:

doing justice, loving covenant faith,
and humbly walking with your God. (Micah 6:6-8)

Yet the historical approach, like the instinctual one, involves a contradiction of a fundamental kind: it contradicts the story itself. While it is true that Isaac is not sacrificed, it is also true that neither Abraham nor God ever repudiates that practice as a grisly abomination. Of course, Abraham does not want to do it. But he never says, "How could I ever have thought this is what God wanted?" God stops Abraham, but he never accuses him of having completely misread the divine mind. As a matter of historical fact, orthodox Israelite faith did abominate child sacrifice; the Prophets attest to this clearly (Jeremiah 7:30-34). But the disorienting thing is that this particular story gives no indication of that position. On the contrary, if *all* we had were this story, then we might reasonably conclude that God admires the practice as a real show of faith. Look, God actually says (through the angel), "By myself I swear—an utterance of the Lord—because you have done this thing and have not withheld your son, your only one—I will indeed bless you and greatly multiply your seed like the stars of the heavens..." (Genesis 22:16-17). The promise of divine blessing is bestowed specifically because of Abraham's willingness to go to this extreme of obedience.

So, as personally involved readers of the Bible, our back is against the wall. The text firmly refuses the historian's kind offer to make God and Abraham look good. And we are not free to say that Abraham's God is not ours. This is, I believe, exactly the position in which the Bible intends to put us, here only a couple of dozen pages into the long and difficult account of Israel's life with God. At the outset of our reading we need to know what kind of God we must reckon with, and what might happen to us in that reckoning. In my view, the story of the Binding of Isaac, far from being sub-

52

Christian, gives us fundamental and crucial information about the God who is the Father of Jesus Christ. Moreover, this information is never eclipsed by the revelation of God in the life, death, and resurrection of Jesus Christ. Just the opposite is true. Without the kind of information about God we begin to gain here, Jesus' death on a cross is more than shocking and tragic: it is nonsensical. (This is why the Binding of Isaac is often chosen as a reading for Good Friday.)

Putting it another way, the essential theological problem—the problem about God—that this story presents does not go away in the New Testament. "Why does God ask for *this*?"—that is one of the abiding questions in Israel's life. Among the stories of the Bible, Genesis 22 and the Passion narratives pose it in the sharpest and most poignant way. They back us up against the wall. For us who cannot get away from the text, the only way out is to read. We must read more slowly than usual, because this is a story in which not a word is wasted, nor casually chosen. As long as we have the patience to stay with the text, it will draw us into its mysteries and reveal to us surprising riches. So let us read.

"And it happened, after these things, that God tested Abraham" (22:1). Our story begins with a backward glance: "after these things." This is not a common introductory phrase in the Old Testament, and so we are moved to ask, "What things?" The narrator is giving us a hint: this stark story, which seems to come out of nowhere and to represent a God who is a stranger to Abraham and to us, does not stand on its own. Getting it in proper perspective depends on remembering the things that came before: the birth of the boy, for instance. This boy who barely escapes immolation by his father is not just any boy (as though there were such a thing). Isaac is the miraculous fruit of barrenness and old age. Sarah was ninety, Abraham one hundred years old when their only son was born. And they had not exactly been enjoying a comfortable retirement. Rather, they had been chasing around the Middle East for twenty-five years now, from Mesopotamia over to Canaan, down to Egypt, and back up again to Canaan—ever since God got Abraham going with that wild demand-and-promise that uprooted him suddenly from everything that was familiar: "*Get you going,* away from your land, and away from your birthplace, and away from your father's house, to the land which I shall show you. And I will make of you a great people, and I will bless you and make your name great. And be a blessing!" (12:1-2). Hear that three-beat measuring of all that Abraham must leave behind: "away from your land, and away from your birthplace, and away from your father's house." We must try to imagine the shock he felt as God hammered the demand home. The worst thing anyone in the ancient world could contemplate was dying way from home—and Abraham was seventy-five when God told him to hit the road. Still worse, for twenty-four years after that there seemed to be not a glimmer of hope that the accompanying promise had any substance. Meantime, Sarah and Abraham endured famine and war and a couple of close calls for Sarah, who was still lovely enough to attract lascivious attention from regional potentates Pharaoh (12:10-17) and Abimelech (20:1-18). Finally, in the twenty-fifth year, the elderly wanderers birth Isaac. At last, they hold in their arms the earnest of God's early promise: "I will make of you a great people."

Very likely those next few years were the happiest the old couple ever knew. For the most part, they were uneventful, as far as the biblical story goes. There was that unpleasant business with Hagar and *her* boy (21:9-21); but apart from that, we know almost nothing about those years. Perhaps there is not much to say about a couple enjoying the simple happiness of raising a child. Then, some time "after these things"—it is not clear exactly how long, maybe a dozen or more years flew past—there came another of those unyielding demands from God: "Take your son, your only one, whom you love, Isaac, and get you going to the land of the Moriah" (22:2). Do you hear it, the same phrase "get you going" that created the first great rupture in Abraham's life? Even the same three-beat rhythm is repeated before the boy is named.

55

The ancient rabbis expand this one terrible verse into a dialogue between God and Abraham. They show us, as the Bible does not, Abraham trying to wiggle out from underneath the divine thumb. Abraham bargains with God for his child's life, as he once bargained for the lives of the faceless Sodomites (18:23-33). Listen to how the desperate father challenges each phrase of God's demand:

"Take your son."

"I have two sons."

"Your only one."

"This one is the only son of his mother, and this (other) one is the only son of his mother."

"The one you love."

"I love them both."

"Isaac."

The rabbinic *midrash*[2] slows down our reading and underscores a peculiarity we might overlook in the shock of the moment. Abraham is trying to exploit a seeming inaccuracy in God's demand, namely, the reference to Abraham's "only son." Abraham, of course, has two sons. Isaac bears the promise of "a great nation" for Abraham, but there is also his first-born, Hagar's son Ishmael, fourteen years older than Isaac (16:16). "Take your son, your only one"—just because the phrase is inappropriate, even offensively so, it draws our attention to one of "these things," to one part of the background of this present event that we should bear in mind. In the previous chapter, Abraham drove Hagar and Ishmael out into the wilderness. There, too, he was meekly responding to a demand, that one from Sarah, who did not want "the son of this slave-woman" (21:10) competing for *her* son's inheritance. And the wording makes it clear that Abraham's actions now mirror his earlier actions. Then, too, he "rose early" (21:14, 22:3); he gathered provisions for the one-way journey and "placed" them on Hagar's shoulder (21:14). Now he "places" on Isaac (22:6) the wood for his own immolation. A few days later, he will "place" Isaac on top of the wood, on the altar (22:9). What is the effect of all these echoes of Ishmael's banishment in the account of Isaac's binding? They underscore the fact that now, as far as Abraham knows, he does have only one son. He has just sent a woman and a child off into the wilderness of the Negev, with a single skin of water. Although he has God's promise that Ishmael will somehow survive to father a distant nation, there is no indication in scripture that Abraham ever sees his first-born son again. Now there is no mistaking the fact that it is upon Isaac alone that the hope for a future rests.

So Abraham saddles the donkey and sets out with two servant lads and his son. His blind obedience to God is, as Kierkegaard says, appalling to watch—like a sleepwalker passing along the edge of an abyss, his footsteps guided only by the instinct of faith. On the third day, they see far off the place God intends, and now the action slows to an excruciating pace. "And Abraham took the wood for the offering and laid it on Isaac, his son, and he took in his hand the fire and the knife" (22:6). Abraham himself carries the dangerous instruments which might harm "his son." "And the two of them walked on together." There is tenderness, intense togetherness in the scene. Over and over the two are named, one in relation to the other, even to the point of narrative awkwardness: "And Isaac said to Abraham, his father, he said, 'My father,' and he said, 'Here I am, my son'" (22:7).

Abraham replies to the boy just as he replied to God at the beginning of the ordeal: "Here I am" (22:1). These words bespeak Abraham's full, unhesitating responsiveness first to God, and now to his son. This is Abraham's agony: to be torn apart by those conflicting responses.

Of course, the Bible does not explicitly tell us that Abraham is torn apart. Biblical narrative is characteristically reticent; it reports only words and actions. Almost never are we given access to someone's feelings and unuttered thoughts. In Marshall McLuhan's terms, the Bible is a very "hot medium." We get involved because the Bible leaves so much imaginative and emotional work for its readers, who must struggle to assimilate this bare report of words and actions. Yet ironically, that very "heat" may be the reason the Bible so often seems boring, at least to modern readers. Movies and television, even modern novels have taught us to expect dramatic scene painting, psychological probing, explosive exchanges. But the Bible tells a story like Rembrandt etches one. You have to slow down and look closely to see much of anything at all, and then let your heart dwell on what you see.

"And Abraham said, 'God will provide himself the sheep for the offering, my son'; and the two of them went on together" (22:8). So much is implied in that sentence: Abraham's tenderness—"my son"; his terrible knowledge, and yet at the same time his faith in God that goes beyond any rational understanding; the helpless intimacy between father and son—"and the two of them went on together." In his old age, Rembrandt became one of the great interpreters of this story. He is great because he sees that intimacy and makes it the key to his rendering of the scene on an etching plate. He had tried his hand at it before. As a young, prodigiously gifted artist, Rembrandt painted a big, flashy canvas that shows a murder in progress: Isaac is sprawled across a rock, chest bare; Abraham is caught just at the point of plunging in the knife; there appears at his side a curly-headed young man, with an urgent look and just a hint of wings. The scene has all the drama anyone could require.

58

But it is a completely different reading of the story that Rembrandt drew later, when he himself had lost children, and was father to an only son. Now Isaac kneels beside the seated Abraham, who is cradling his head, covering the boy's eyes with one hand. An older woman, gazing at this etching, said, "If I had to kill my child, this is how I would do it." This time the angel stands behind Abraham with wings outspread. If Rembrandt earlier painted a barely divine messenger boy, now he draws a strong, sheltering figure, who cradles Abraham as he cradles his son. This is the moment of release from God's demand. But it comes too late for Abraham to feel relief. He seems not even to see the angel, nor does he look at the boy. He has the unfocused stare, the ravaged expression of someone who has survived something unspeakable. Rembrandt shows us just what it costs Abraham to be fully responsive to God and fully responsive to his son. It costs, in T. S. Eliot's phrase, "not less than everything."[3]

Among those who do not try to do an end-run around this story but accept it on its own terms, the Binding of Isaac is regarded as the signal biblical instance of human obedience and unquestioning faith. Abraham passes the loyalty test. Yet Rembrandt's portrait reminds us that there is no relief for Abraham at the end of this story. Rather, there is a terrible question about God. Genesis is primarily a book about God, and secondarily about human beings encountering God. So we have to ask, what does this story tell us about God? Can we honestly say anything other than, "This is an archaic story of God the Tyrant, who dangles Abraham from

a hook and watches him squirm until the divine ego is satisfied, then lets him go and waits for a big thank-you"?

Here in the Bible, all we have to guide us in answering the
question about God are the words. The words of the story do
express a kind of relief—yet not Abraham's relief, but God's:

59

> And God said, "Do not lay your hand on the lad; do
> not do a thing to him. *For now I know* that you are a
> God-fearer; and you have not withheld your son, your
> only one, from me." (22:12)

God knows something now that God did not know before.
Genesis offers little support for a doctrine of divine omnis-
cience, if by that we mean that God knows everything we are
going to do before we do it. One of the medieval rabbinic
commentators on this verse observes wisely: "God can only
know things that can be known."[4] And the free response of
the human will is not a thing that can be known, with any
certainty, in advance. So when God tests Abraham, it is a real
test. This ghastly ordeal, one time only in the history of the
world, was designed particularly to give God certain and
crucial information about this man Abraham. The test will
show whether he cares about God above everything and
everyone else—even above Isaac, Abraham's "only" son and
his one hope for seeing God's promise fulfilled.

But why should Abraham be singled out thus, to be tested in a way no one else in the Bible is tested, before or since?
That is the question we need to answer in order to make
sense of this uniquely terrifying event. And again, the words
give us a clue. The narrative begins by reminding us that this
most extreme of all tests occurs at a particular time in the
history of the world. "*After these things,* God tested
Abraham" (22:1)—after a lot of difficult experience for
Abraham, as we have already seen, but also after a lot of difficult experience for God. Think for a moment how the his-

THE COST OF LOVE

tory of humankind up to this point must look, seen from
God's perspective: the betrayal in the garden in the first generation, the murder of a brother in the second, the rapid
escalation of violence so that the whole earth becomes filled
with it (Genesis 6:12). With the flood, God resolves to make
a clean sweep, but nothing really changes after that, as the
Tower of Babel incident shows. The first eleven chapters of
Genesis—the "Primeval History," from the Garden of Eden
to the Tower of Babel—is predominantly a story of steady
alienation from God, human rejection of God. And so in
chapter 12, with the calling of Abraham, God tries a new
strategy. At this point, God gives up on trying to work a
blessing directly upon all humankind. From now on, God
will work through one man, one family, one people, in order
to reach all people. The global scope of Abraham's call is evident from the beginning: "I will bless those who bless you,
and the one who curses you, I will curse. And *through you* all
the families of the earth shall experience blessing" (12:3).
Abraham and his seed—henceforth this is the prism through
which God's blessing is to be diffused through the whole
world.

The old strategy did not work. But God's new strategy is
hardly surefire. We should not be surprised if adopting it
makes God anxious, for now everything depends on the
faithfulness of this one man Abraham. God, having been
badly and repeatedly burned by human sin throughout the
first chapters of Genesis yet still passionately desirous of
working blessing in the world, now chooses to become totally vulnerable on the point of this one man's faithfulness. It is,
to say the least, a counter-intuitive solution to a problem.
And now, ten chapters into the saga of God and Abraham,
God has further reason to be anxious. For a shadow of doubt
has fallen over Abraham's total faith in God. Twice it is
recorded that Abraham has Sarah pass herself off as his sis-

ter. In Egypt (Genesis 12:10-16) and again in Canaan (20:1-18), he lets his beautiful wife go into a king's harem rather than trusting her to God's protection on their sojourn. As feminist interpreters have helped us see, it is a disappointing showing for God's best man.

We have to take all these things into account in order to make heart-sense of this appalling test, to see why God would go to this length to know for sure whether the single human thread upon which blessing hangs will hold firm. God is totally vulnerable in this matter of Abraham. It is noteworthy that we are given no indication at all of what Abraham may have felt when the test was over; he just goes home (22:19). But God's relief erupts from the page. It is huge, global: "And all the nations of the earth shall find blessing through your seed, because you heeded my voice" (22:18). The fate of the cosmos, God's dream for all the world, was teetering in the balance as Abraham and Isaac were climbing the mountain.

This may be the most difficult story in the whole Bible. So why does it occur so near the beginning? We could never completely understand the Binding of Isaac even if it were reported on the last page. Why, then, does the Bible take the risk of putting us off God at the outset, when we are just getting our feet wet? We know, in fact, that many readers never really get past this story; they consider that this is all they need to know about "the God of the Old Testament." And that reaction is not entirely wrong—mostly wrong perhaps, but not entirely. I am convinced that this story appears only twenty-two chapters into the Bible because it tells us, not *everything* we need to know, but something fundamental about the God of Israel. And the sooner we learn this, then the more headway we are likely to make in comprehending and accepting Israel's complex witness to that God. The more headway we are likely to make in our own relationship with Gòd. So the risk must be taken.

The Binding of Isaac shows us a God who is vulnerable, terribly and terrifyingly so, in the context of covenant relationship. We are more comfortable using the "omni" words— omnipotent, omniscient—to describe God. Yet if we properly understand the dynamics of covenant relationship, then we are confronted with a God who is vulnerable. For, as both Testaments maintain, the covenant with God is fundamentally an unbreakable bond of love (*ḥesed*). And ordinary experience teaches that love and vulnerability are inextricably linked; we are most vulnerable to emotional pain when the well-being and the faithfulness of those we love are at stake. And as we have seen, the Bible shows that the faithfulness of even the best of God's covenant partners is always up for grabs. So it follows that God's vulnerability in love is an essential element of covenant relationship.

Two sources in the Christian tradition confirm the notion that God is painfully vulnerable with respect to the faithfulness of those on whom God counts most. First, there are important parallels between this story and the final resurrection appearance in the gospel of John, when our Lord asks Peter, "Simon (son) of John, do you love me more than these?" (John 21:15). The thrice-repeated question is normally treated as an opportunity for Peter to rehabilitate himself after his threefold denial of his Lord. That makes sense, from Peter's side, but what about from Jesus' side? To put it crudely, what might be our crucified Lord's interest in pressing that question so hard?

Peter is the Rock on which the church is to be built (Matthew 16:18). God in Christ depends on him for the dissemination of divine blessing, just as God depended on Abraham. "Do you love me?...Do you love me?...Do you love me?" Were it any other speaker, we would not hesitate to recognize poignancy in the question, and anxious doubt, especially following a betrayal. Surely that is just what it is: the question pressed by Jesus is another expression of divine vulnerability. And again, as with the testing of Abraham, the only thing that makes the terrible human cost tolerable is the urgency of God's need to be sure of love—a genuine or (dare we say it?) forgivable need. Peter verbally asserts his love three times, and then his Lord tells him how he must show it:

> This I have to tell you in solemn truth. When you were young, you would fasten your girdle around you and go wherever you chose. But when you have grown old, you will stretch our your hands, and it will be a stranger who will be girding you up and carrying you off to a place where you have no wish to go. (John 21: 18)

Tradition has it that Peter died hung upside down on a cross.

A second source of confirmation for this reading of the Binding of Isaac is the fact that the church has always found here a foreshadowing of Jesus' Passion; the story is often read on Good Friday. On that day, it is obviously appropriate to hear this story that tells first, of a father's selfless willingness to sacrifice a beloved son, and second, of total human faithfulness to God. But if, as I believe, this story testifies to God's extreme vulnerability to human unfaithfulness, then we can say more about its appropriateness to Good Friday. It is in Christ hanging on the cross that we see, for once in history, the two sides of this story fully joined in one person. In Jesus Christ we see a son of Abraham sparing nothing, totally faithful in covenant relationship with God. At the same time, we see in Jesus God's total faithfulness, expressed now as excruciating vulnerability, even to death on a cross. These two images—Abraham binding Isaac, Christ nailed on a cross—are the supporting structures for the long and convoluted story of sin and salvation. When reason fails, as it does at least one Friday each year, then we must listen to the stories with our hearts.

64

Notes

1. The Binding of Isaac is the common name for the story in Jewish tradition. I choose it over the common Christian designation, the Sacrifice of Isaac, because it more accurately reflects what does and does not happen in the story.

2. The Hebrew term *midrash* denotes an imaginative expansion of scripture; this is the most common form of biblical interpretation in Jewish tradition.

3. The phrase comes from the last few lines of *Four Quartets:* "A condition of complete simplicity (costing not less than everything)..." ("Little Gidding," V).

4. Gersonides (Ralbag), *Miqra'ot Gedolot,* ad loc.

CHAPTER SEVEN

"THE ONE WHOM MY SOUL LOVES"

The Song of Songs

HERE IS A BOOK that barely (no pun intended) made it into the Bible, and with good reason. It never mentions God, at least not explicitly, and it mentions a lot of other things we would not expect to find in the Bible. The scriptural status of the Song of Songs is so questionable that the Talmud actually records the great debate that occurred at the end of the first century, when the rabbis of Roman Palestine were making final decisions about what was in the canon of authoritative writings, and what was out. It was the declamation of Rabbi Akiba, the great teacher, scholar, and martyr of early Judaism, that finally carried the day:

> Heaven forbid! No Jew ever questioned the sanctity of the Song of Songs; for all the world is not worth the day when the Song of Songs was given to Israel. For all the Writings are holy, but the Song of Songs is the Holy of Holies![1]

It is not quite true that "no Jew ever questioned the sanctity of the Song of Songs." In fact, it seems to have acquired some popularity as a drinking song in the Palestinian pubs, and that is probably why Akiba pronounces its sanctity so forcefully. Elsewhere the Talmud records his equally stern warning: "Anyone who trills his voice in singing the Song of Songs in the banquet house or treats it as some kind of tune has no part in the world to come!"[2]

Akiba's view of the Song's unique holiness carried not only that day, but well over a millennium of biblical interpretation among both Jews and Christians. The eight chapters of the Song of Songs have generated more commentary than almost any other book of the Bible. Indeed, the first biblical commentary ever written was *On the Song of Songs,* by the third-century Christian Origen. His sermons on the same book are among the earliest sermons preserved outside the Bible itself. The medieval church riveted its attention on the Song. More than a hundred commentaries and doubtless thousands of sermons were produced as the monastic theologians explored every facet of this text, which they read as the consummate celebration of the love binding God and the church, or God and the mystic's soul. In the thirteenth century, Bernard wrote eighty-six sermons on the Song of Songs, and he never got beyond chapter three, verse one!

In recent years, however, the tide of interpretation has turned. Once more, this small book is generating an abundance of commentary vastly disproportionate to its size, yet almost all modern commentators agree that the traditional view is wholly arbitrary and completely wrong. The present consensus is that the Song is a celebration of human sexuality that was included in the canon of scripture by a happy mistake, because the ancient rabbis thought it was about the love between God and Israel. If these commentators are correct, then this must be the biggest religious joke of all time, beating any story you could dream up about a rabbi and a priest in a rowboat or on a golf course. And the joke is sadly on us, the modern readers of the Bible, because it means that what has traditionally been seen as the Song's distinctive *theological* contribution to the canon is missing altogether. If the Song is solely a celebration of human love, then nowhere within the covers of the Bible is there a truly happy story about God and Israel (or God and the church) in love. Sure, there is divine love in abundance: saving love, unrequited love, tortured love, Love dying on a cross, love that cannot die. There is even human love expressed for God: "I love you, O LORD, my strength" (Psalm 18:2)—although somewhat less of that. But each of these is in a sense a one-sided expression of love. If the Song has nothing to do with the story of God and Israel after all, then there is nowhere to turn to hear one partner say, "I love you," and the other answer right back, "Yes, yes; I love you, too." For this is the only place in the Bible where there is a *dialogue* of love. Indeed, in this respect the Song of Songs is unparalleled in the whole literature of the ancient Near East, as far as we know. And if that unique dialogue between God and Israel is just an ancient rabbinical invention, then we must accept the sad fact that there is at the heart of the Bible a cosmic loneliness that finds no relief.

However, there is a great deal of evidence indicating that indeed "the Song of Songs is the Holy of Holies." In highly imaginative fashion, the Song captures the ecstatic aspect of the love that is the main subject of the whole Bible. Yet one must also ask, Is there no case to be made for a sexual interpretation? Even if Akiba was right that crooning the Song of Songs in a bar is an infernally bad idea (and I think he has a point), does that then mean that its blatant eroticism is a kind of elaborate snow job, a trap designed to confound the wicked?

If the Song of Songs is about the love between God and Israel and has *nothing* to do with sexual love, then that interpretation, too, leaves a gaping hole in the canon. For the Bible then lacks any strong statement about love between man and woman enjoyed in full mutuality and equality of status. There are some only-too-clear biblical statements tending in the opposite direction; they indicate that in our fallen world, mutuality and equality are not the norm. Indeed, loss of equality in sexual relationship is the immediate outcome of "the Fall" in Eden: "And to the woman [God] said, '... toward your husband will be your desire, but it is he who will rule over you!'" (Genesis 3:16). If that is the primeval reality, then Ephesians 5 indicates that nothing had greatly changed by the time of Christ: "Just as the church is subject to Christ, so also wives ought to be, in everything, to their husbands." The Pauline writer is grappling with "a great mystery" about Christ and the church (5:32), but in this matter of family dynamics his vision does not go beyond the social reality of the Roman Empire.

I am persuaded, on the basis of evidence both internal to the text and external to it, that the Song is talking about happiness in both respects, in divine love and in sexual love, and talking about more besides (as I shall discuss at the end of this chapter). First, the internal evidence. Two things are striking about the language of the Song. The most obvious of these is, of course, its use of erotic language. But equally striking is the fact that the Song is in large part (erotica included) a mosaic of quotations from other parts of scripture. Phrases from the Prophets, the Torah, and the Psalms abound. I do not mean just scattered words, but in many cases connected phrases—vivid images and terms too specific for their other contexts to be forgotten by those familiar with biblical language. The Song is like an echo chamber, and modern commentators have not taken that phenomenon seriously enough. We need an interpretation of the Song that takes full account of its remarkable scriptural resonance, which *cannot be separated from the erotic language.*

The argument for the connection between divine love and sexual love can be made on grounds external to the text as well. A holistic understanding of our own humanity suggests that our religious capacity is linked with an awareness of our sexuality. *Fundamental to both is a desire to transcend the confines of the self for the sake of intimacy with the other.* Sexual love provides many people with their first experience of ecstasy, which literally means "standing outside oneself." Therefore the experience of healthy sexual desire can help us imagine what it might mean to love God truly—a less natural feeling for many of us, especially in our secular society. On the other hand, from what the Bible tells us about God's love for us, we can come to recognize sexual love as an arena for the formation of the soul. Like the love of God, profound love of another person demands devotion of the whole self, and the steady practice of repentance and forgiveness. Sooner or later, it requires of us suffering and sacrifice. A full reading of the Song of Songs stretches our minds to span categories of experience that our modern intellects too neatly separate. Accordingly, we need a style of interpretation that allows the text to mean more than one thing at the same time.

Standing on Even Ground
We must begin, just as the medieval monks did, hearing ourselves addressed by the text at the level of experience that is most familiar to us. Putting it another way, we must begin at the level where we are currently striving, more or less consciously, for insight. That is where the word of God can enter our hearts, and then perhaps open us up to levels of experience we had never imagined that we could achieve or even

desire. For the monks, the familiar arena was contemplative experience; for most of us, it is sexual experience. So what, then, does the Song tell us?

Above all, it tells us about woman and man facing one another on even ground, each speaking with frank admiration about the other's beauty and power. Interestingly, the most memorable images of power are the man's compliments to the woman:

> I compare you, my love,
> to a mare among Pharaoh's chariots....
> Your neck is like the tower of David, built in courses;
> on it hang a thousand bucklers, all of them shields
> of warriors. (1:9; 4:4)

The first comparison is no casual compliment. Rather, it shows the poet's good knowledge of history. Pharaoh's chariots were drawn by stallions, not mares. But once, when Pharaoh was at war with the Prince of Qadesh, the enemy drove a mare in heat out into the midst of his chariotry, with the predictable result. The compliment may therefore be "translated": "You drive strong males wild!"[3]

However, this woman does not need these compliments to boost a faltering ego, nor does she wait for them. The Song is unique among the books of the Bible in that here the woman's voice takes the lead. She speaks first and last, and altogether more than does the man. Yet far more significant than the quantity of her speech is its character. No other woman in scripture speaks with this measure of self-confidence; no one else asks so boldly for what she wants: "Let him kiss me with the kisses of his mouth!" And then, addressing her lover directly: "For better is your lovemaking than wine!" (1:2). This woman already has "a healthy self-image"; she sees herself as something lovely: "I am a rose of the Sharon [Valley], a lily of the valleys" (2:1). And her lover agrees: "Like a rose among thorns, so is my friend (*ra'yatî*) among maidens" (2:2). The lovers often share words and metaphors in this way; one echoes and amplifies the other's "sweet nothings." This intertwined speech is one of the most appealing features of the Song, and also one of the most realistic; it is how lovers talk in their most private moments.

Ra'yatî, he calls her, "my friend, my companion": this is the man's customary term of endearment for the woman. We do not have another indication in scripture of an Israelite man addressing his lover thus. It may even have sounded surprising to ancient ears. The same term in masculine grammatical form (here it is feminine) normally denotes a fellow Israelite, someone to whom covenant obligation is due, a "neighbor": "You shall love your neighbor as yourself" (Leviticus 19:18). Calling a lover a "friend" in this sense might seem unromantic, even disappointing. But on deeper reflection, the term appears to be carefully chosen in order to convey the highest regard, a regard that may begin with romantic feeling and yet transcends it.

Appearing in the context of scripture, *ra'yatî* is a term of endearment that implies covenantal relationship. In other words, the excited young lovers are bound together not only by immediate affection, but also by God's intention for their relationship. Calling her "my neighbor, my companion," the man is (unconsciously?) conforming his understanding of the relationship to God's dream for the human being at the beginning of the world: "It is not good for the human (*'adam*) to be by himself. I shall make for him a help[4] *corresponding to him.*" God's dream for the human is that woman and man should be equal and complementary, for they are equally created as "the image of God" (Genesis 1:27).

There is one place in the Song that makes it unmistakably clear that the long sad history of asymmetry between man and woman is a thing of the past, and a new paradigm is

71

being established. In Eden, it seemed that the woman's own sexual desire condemned her to subordination: "toward your husband will be your desire (*t'shuqah*), but it is he who will rule over you!" (Genesis 3:16). But here, after a lengthy exchange of poetic compliments (5:10–7:10), the woman exults: "I am for my lover, and toward me is *his* desire (*t'shuqah*)!" (7:11). Because that word *t'shuqah* is a rare one, occurring only here in the Song and in Genesis (3:16 and 4:7), the line the poet is drawing stands out clearly. This is an intentional echo and a reversal of the sad ending of the idyll in Eden. No longer, the poem declares, are desire and power unequally distributed between woman and man. The woman proclaims a true partnership of unrestrained self-giving and mutual advocacy: "I am for my darling and he is for me"[5] (6:3, compare 2:16).

So the Song of Songs is a radical poem in the truest sense. It digs down to roots (Latin *radices*), to the very base of history, and works for repair and renewal. And it does this in the only way a poem can work, with words. Here the poet has chosen a word, *t'shuqah* (desire), that carries the mind steeped in biblical language back to the dawn of time. The composer of the Song is a religious poet in the same style as T. S. Eliot.[6] It is her (?)[7] habit to take old words from the religious tradition and set them in new contexts, where they acquire fresh associations. She is consciously rereading the tradition, at the same time creating a continuation and a turning point in that tradition. She is witnessing to the new possibility that she sees God creating with this man and this woman.

The word *t'shuqah* stands in the "old" biblical tradition, in Genesis, as a red flag warning: "Caution, danger for women! Love may be hazardous to your health, to your *shalôm*, your peace of mind and body." Evidently the word was so laden with bad associations that no one touched it again for centuries; it appears nowhere in the many pages and centuries between Genesis and the Song of Songs. But now at last a woman in love rejoices: "I am for my lover, and toward me is his *t'shuqah!*" A rose replaces the red flag. The word now marks a new beginning to sexual history, a place of healing for women and men together.

A Handle on the Torah
The ancient rabbis noticed that it was the practice of this poet (of course, they called the poet of the Song "Solomon") to reuse old words from the scriptural tradition. They understood that the Song represents a rereading of the tradition, and they expressed that relation in an evocative metaphor:

> Torah is like a basket full of fruits, which had no handle, and it could not be carried. And someone wise came and made for it handles, and it began to be carried by its handles. So until Solomon came, no one could understand the words of Torah, but once Solomon had been, everyone began to comprehend Torah.[8]

The "handles" Rabbi Yose describes are the three books traditionally attributed to Solomon: the Song of Songs, Proverbs, and Ecclesiastes. In other words, these three books, which speak so profoundly of the ordinary things of life, give us access to the divine mysteries of Torah.

As the *midrash* continues with a new metaphor, our understanding of the relationship between the Torah and the Solomonic books deepens:

> Rabbi Hanina said, [Torah] is like a deep well full of water, and its waters were cold and sweet and good; but no one could drink of them. Someone came and provided a rope [tied] to a rope, a cord [tied] to a cord, and he drew from it and he drank. Thus all

began to draw and drink. So from word to word, from *mashal* [a figurative saying or metaphor] to *mashal*, Solomon comprehended the secret of Torah, as it is written, "The *meshalîm* of Solomon the son of David, King of Israel" [Proverbs 1:1]. By virtue of his *meshalîm*, Solomon comprehended the words of Torah.

"From word to word, from metaphor to metaphor, Solomon comprehended the secret of Torah." With wonderful economy, the rabbis are describing exactly how the Song effects its rereading of the tradition: a word here echoes a word there, a metaphor here sends us searching through memory to locate other occurrences of the image. Like reading Eliot, reading the Song with full attention is a slow business. It is as if all of history is passing before our eyes. And this is, I think, exactly what the poet of the Song intended.

The Song of Songs represents a total revisioning of human history. That is why, through the medium of allusive language, it takes us back to the Garden of Eden. From a biblical perspective, the main lines of history were laid down in Eden, when humanity "fell" into the world as we know it. The third chapter of the Bible shows the outcome of the first human disobedience, and the divine speech there is a remarkable social and ecological exposé. The original harmony of creation is torn apart. Ruptures are visible at three levels. First, woman and man are divided, by blame and then by an imbalance of power. Second, hostile separations occur between humans and the non-human world. Woman's seed and snake's seed from now on will exist in enmity (Genesis 3:15). Further, "Thorn and briar will spring up *for you*" (3:18). There is more than a hint of divine sarcasm as the original pleasant task of watching the fertile soil produce food[9] turns into the grunt work of hoeing weeds. But the most far-reaching damage is at the third level: the trusting intimacy between God and humanity, which was to have been a source of perpetual blessing on both sides (see also Genesis 1:28), is shattered.

Yet the poet of the Song has a dream, and in that dream all the ruptures that occurred in Eden are repaired. This poem resembles more than anything else the account of a dream. The symbolic language is suggestive but elusive; scenes shift without logical connection. Each detail cannot be identified with precision: interpreting the Song, like making sense of a dream, is an exercise in associative thinking. Nonetheless, following carefully and imaginatively where the words of the Song lead, we can share the poet's and God's dream of the original harmony of creation restored at all these levels. A woman and a man, equally powerful, are lost in admiration of one another—or more accurately, in admiration they truly find themselves and each other. And the natural world rejoices with them. Instead of the sadly familiar thorn and briar, flowers and fruits spring up in exotic profusion—a paradise. Nowhere in the known world do all these plants bloom together; here they bloom with an exuberance that mirrors the lovers' own.

Less obvious is the healing that occurs at the third level, between God and humanity. Maybe the very fact that it is *not* obvious reflects the realism that is such a consistent element of biblical literature. For if a dream of God is a delicate thing, how much more so a dream of God the Lover. With exquisite delicacy, the poet of the Song chooses words that create intricate patterns of resonance with the religious tradition. If our ears are attuned to biblical idiom, and if we are open to sharing a dream of God, then we may hear them—although it must be admitted that they are often difficult to catch when reading the Song in translation. There are dozens, probably hundreds of words that participate in these patterns.[10] Sometimes the close reader has the sense of having slipped through the looking glass. We find ourselves in a place we did not expect to be, and could not have reached on the strength of our own imagination. Then, perhaps, the Holy Spirit is whispering sweet nothings in our ears.

In this example, the woman is speaking:

> Upon my bed by night I sought
> *the one whom my soul loves.*
> I sought him and did not find him.
> Let me arise now and go about in the city,
> in the streets and in the plazas,
> let me seek *the one whom my soul loves.*
> I sought him and did not find him.
> The guards found me,
> the ones going about the city.
> "*The one whom my soul loves*—have you seen him?"
> Scarcely had I departed from them
> than I found *the one whom my soul loves.*
> I grabbed him and would not let him go....
>
> (3:1-4)

"The one whom my soul loves": this is not the language normally used in filing a missing-persons report—the ostensible occasion for the speech. Yet such an odd phrase cannot be just a slip of the tongue: it is repeated here four times, even to the point of awkwardness. This gifted poet is willingly sacrificing elegance in order to focus attention on a phrase that does not suit its present context very well. But suppose that is just the point. The phrase sounds out of place, but four repetitions are sufficient to recall another context where similar language seems completely *in* place. In the context of Torah, "the One whom [the] soul loves" is, of course, God. The phrase in the Song could be heard as a shortened form of "the first and great commandment": "And you shall *love*

the LORD your God with all your heart and with all your *soul*
and with all your might" (Deuteronomy 6:5).

This repeated echo of the weightiest verse in Torah gives
substance to the scene of the woman urgently seeking the
soul's beloved. Further, the theme of seeking itself has religious resonance. "Seeking God" is a technical term for going
to the sanctuary (Exodus 33:7), or for turning to God in
repentance. The Deuteronomist promises those in exile:
"And you will seek the LORD your God from there [exile] and
you will find him, when you seek him with all your heart and
with all your soul" (Deuteronomy 4:29). The Song "puts a
handle" on that promise of Torah. It enables us to feel what
it is like to seek God with a whole soul, and it reminds us that
God is not, after all, an easy catch. There is hard-won victory in the woman's statement, "I grabbed him and would not
let him go."

Solomon tied "metaphor to metaphor," the rabbis said.
When the Song is connected to the dominant metaphors of
the Bible, there is nothing arbitrary about finding within it
references to a passionate love affair between Israel and God.
For the prophets regularly characterize God's relations with
Israel in terms of courtship and marriage—along with adultery, divorce, and difficult reconciliation. That the Old
Testament represents God chiefly as angry Judge and vicious
Warrior is a false stereotype. While these images are not
absent, they are more than balanced by striking portrayals of
God as Lover or Husband, infatuated with Israel beyond all
reason or deserving. God is not too proud to grieve terribly
over Israel's unfaithfulness, nor to be giddy over her return
home. These "undignified" portrayals reveal that Israel's
covenant with God, like human marriage,[11] is only secondarily a legal arrangement. Its primary quality is love at the
highest pitch of intensity. Of course, the covenant can only
work well if love is strong on both sides. The recurrent

tragedy of biblical history is that human love and responsiveness to God repeatedly weaken and fail. And the Song of Songs, this poem of happy love, is honest enough to deal with that problem.

78

In another scene the woman is lying in bed, recounting the nighttime visit of her lover:[12]

> I sleep but my heart is awake—the sound of my
>   darling knocking!
> "Open to me, my sister, my friend (ra'yatî), my dove,
>   my perfect one.
> For my head is covered with dew, my locks with
>   drops of night."

And she replies:

> "I have taken off my dress: how can I put it on again?
> I have washed my feet: how can I dirty them?"
> My darling thrust his hand from the opening,
> and *my guts churned for him*. (5:2-4)

"My guts churned for him"—this is infelicitous, but the Hebrew (*me'aî hamû*) is not delicate. Translators generally try to make this sound more like typical love language: "my inmost being yearned for him" (NRSV); "my heart was stirred for him" (NJPS).[13] But the woman's words are more elemental than that: *me'aî* are "innards, intestines, guts."

Most modern commentators see this as a clear sexual reference. One even identifies the heaving part of the female anatomy as the "bulbospongiosus muscle." This strikes me as the kind of information that is inconsequential even if accurate. What is generally overlooked is the fact that this phrase is a quotation from the prophet Jeremiah. Listen to the way Jeremiah represents God, yearning for the Northern Kingdom of Israel, destroyed a hundred years before Jeremiah's birth:

Is not Ephraim a beloved son to me, a cuddled child?
Oh, whenever I speak of him, I remember him all
    over again.
Therefore *my guts churn for him;*
surely I will have mercy upon him, says the LORD.
"Turn back, virgin Israel....
How long will you *turn yourself away,* turnabout
    daughter?" (Jeremiah 31:19, 21)

79

This is not an easy passage to forget, once you have heard
it.[14] Multiple echoes of rare and memorable words[15] indicate
that the composer of the Song remembers the Jeremiah passage and expects her audience to remember it. And to what
purpose? Now the "woman"—let us say, Israel—feels the
kind of gut-churning love that God has felt. But no happy
ending yet. Too late she gets up to answer the knock:

I opened, I, to my darling,
but my darling *had turned away,* departed. (5:6)

This aborted encounter is followed by another search scene.
She does not find him, and so she tells the daughters of
Jerusalem:

If *you* find my darling—what should you tell him?
That I am sick with love. (5:8)

That lovesickness acquires poignancy and depth if we con-
nect it with Israel's striving to return to God. It suggests: This
time, we *almost* made it.

When commentators treat the Song solely as a human
love story, they rarely observe that it is not, upon close reading, a poem of love fulfilled. If the lovers do live "happily ever
after," we never hear about it. To the very end they both
express intense yearning, anticipation rather than satisfaction. It is telling that the final word (spoken by the woman)
bespeaks separation between the lovers: "Flee, my darling,

80

and be like a gazelle or a young stag on the spice mountains!" (8:14). She may well be urging him to flee his companions and come to her. But she also could be cautioning him to run *away* (the normal meaning of the Hebrew verb); perhaps the garden is not yet wholly safe for love. In either case, the Song ends with the lovers not nestled together, but unsettled, ever in motion—like Keats's lovers on the Grecian urn, their love "For ever warm and still to be enjoyed." Thus the Song realistically portrays the condition of young love. Is it not also a true reflection of the best we can expect, as long as we are in this world, of our life with God?

Practical Mysticism and the Song of Songs

The Song of Songs ends with the longing for intimacy yet to be wholly satisfied. Endings are important in all books, but the biblical writers have a particular genius for them. Rarely, if ever, do they leave things tied up neatly, with nothing more to be hoped for or desired. Characteristically, they leave us in the middle of some situation with a long way to go before the end of the journey is reached. Although we may be uncertain, nevertheless we have been given direction, disposed toward a certain kind of striving in our life with God.

The fact that the Song leaves us yearning for intimacy is a matter of the greatest religious significance. Its distinctive contribution to the message of scripture is that genuine intimacy brings us into contact with the sacred. That is why the Song of Songs is often read at wedding ceremonies, even by people who have no notion that it may have anything directly to do with God. Intimacy is the means whereby human life in this world is sanctified. No generation has stood more in need of that affirmation than the present one. Our world is groaning under the burdens of instantaneous contacts and temporary relationships, high mobility, commitments lightly undertaken and readily set aside. Too many souls are stunted, arrested in permanent adolescence. This is true with regard to sexual relations, and also in the other areas of human experience to which the Song points: religious experience and relations between humans and the natural world. Though our wounds in these three areas go back to Eden, still many would agree that the illness has now reached crisis proportions.

The cultivation of real intimacy—with God, with other humans, with the creatures—is the greatest social and spiritual challenge of our time. Precisely because it addresses us in the language of yearning, not satisfaction, the Song can help us grow to meet that challenge. Unhealthy yearning—greed, lust—may destroy us and even the planet, as we are now beginning to recognize. But there is immense healing power in yearning for the *shalôm* (health, wholeness, peace) for which we were created. The Song can guide us because it expresses our deepest desire and seeks to direct it toward healing in all these areas.

I am suggesting that contemporary Christians and Jews need to understand the Song as it has traditionally been understood and used in those traditions—namely, as a mystical text. In our culture, mysticism is sadly misunderstood and maligned as disconnected with reality: impractical at best and dangerously irresponsible at worst. Even those who may admire mysticism often regard it as the special capacity of a few spiritually gifted people, almost all of whom lived in the Middle Ages. But that is a misconception, and a dangerous one in light of our present situation. Mysticism is not an escape from reality, but the opposite. It is a prayerful penetration of reality, guided by both the imagination and the scriptures—which address themselves in such large part to the imagination.

The biblical term for the imaginative capacity is "heart," something with which everyone is equipped. So mysticism is not the province of the chosen few. Rather, this "heart-knowledge" of God and the world that God has made is within the reach of every thinking person. And because mystical thinking allows us to penetrate reality more deeply than we normally do, it is a highly practical skill for a person, a church, or a society in crisis. I believe that the Song of Songs can help us develop the sort of mystical sensibility that may lead to our healing in every sphere.

First, and most obviously, the Song affirms the incomparable joy of faithful sexual relationship. Thus its message is a direct challenge to our society's infatuation with constant newness, even in sexual partners. A sophisticated urban woman, now married after many years of a "single lifestyle," reflects: "I never realized how lush sex could be, when each of you knows for sure that you are the only one." Images throughout the Song underscore the lushness of sexual exclusivity: "I come to my garden, my sister, my bride. . . . My dove, my perfect one, is the only one" (5:1, 6:9). In some social settings the devaluing of devoted sexuality is literally epidemic. In inner cities in North America, for example, single-parent homes have become the norm. An African-American pastor uses the Song of Songs as a basic teaching text for the men in her congregation, asserting: "To us, it speaks an essential evangelical message: 'Cherishing your wife is manly; giving her respect and pleasure—that's cool.'"

At a second level of reading, the Song affirms that longing for intimacy with God is a necessary desire for a healthy soul. Even regular church-goers are not generally conscious of this desire, and therefore do not nurture it. There are two kinds of love of God, both of them good. The more common kind is the grateful love that we feel in response to our countless experiences of God's mercy, generosity, and blessing. This is the love that prompts us to murmur, when things turn out better than we dared hope, "Thank God!"

But there is another love that is even more precious. It arises in us not from anything God has *done* for us, but spontaneously, because our souls were made to delight simply in God's being, and God's being with us. One great modern mystic, Rav (Rabbi) Abraham Isaac Kook, taught that all the rich imagery of the Song of Songs exists precisely for the sake of making vividly real this rare love that does not derive from material benefits.[16] The Song shows us love in its purest form. This is the only place in the Bible where the love between man and woman is celebrated without regard for childbearing or other "utilitarian" benefits of marriage. Of course, in the real world all love, including love of God, is inevitably touched by an awareness of practical benefits. Perhaps this is why the Song takes the form of a dream, with no clear story line—despite attempts of numerous commentators to give it one. The words of the lovers are not embedded in any narrative; they are, in a sense, "out of this world." The Song shows us only isolated moments of pure desire and delight in the presence of the other.

What is not obvious and yet is pervasive in the Song is the way it evokes a healed relationship between humanity and the natural world. Notice a curious feature: for all the long descriptive passages in the poem, we never get a clear picture of what the lovers look like. I can easily summon a mental image of Helen of Troy and Paris, or Tristan and Isolde—but not this pair. In fact, the poem does not even tempt me to imagine what they might *really* look like. Descriptions such as these discourage realistic reconstruction:

> My darling is like a gazelle or a young stag.
> Here he is standing behind our wall....
> Your teeth are like a flock of shorn ewes that come
>   up from the washing;
> all of them bear twins, and there is none among
>   them bereaved. (2:9; 4:2)

Yet a picture does arise in my mind—not of a terrific looking woman and man, but of a lush land bursting with spring:

> My darling speaks and says to me:
> "Rise, my friend; my beauty, come now.
> For lo, the winter is past;
> the rain has finished and gone.
> The blossoms appear on the earth;
> the time of singing has arrived,
> and the voice of the turtledove is heard in our land."
>
> Come, my darling, let us go out to the fields.
> Let us spend the night in the villages.
> We will go early to the vineyards
> and see if the vines have flowered,
> whether the grape blossoms have opened,
> the pomegranates bloomed.
> There I will give you my loving. (2:10-12; 7:12-13)

The body of the man or woman and the lush landscape fuse in our imaginations; they become at points interchangeable as objects of love:

> His cheeks are like beds of spices,
> rich with fragrance. (5:13)

> Your hair is like a flock of goats, tumbling down
>   from Mount Gilead. (4:2)

> You are beautiful as Tirzah, my friend,
> comely as Jerusalem,
> daunting as bannered cities. (6:4)

Certainly this "confusion" between beloved person and land is strange, from our western perspective. One modern rendering of the Song into English removes most of the geographic references, so that the Song appears as universal love poetry of a more conventional style. The only problem with this approach is that it does not sound much like the Song of Songs.

But suppose we take seriously that blurred boundary between beloved body and beloved land, and ask what revelatory value such *un*conventional language may have for us. If this is radical, mystical poetry that aims to restore the intimate relationships fundamental to our humanity, then we must discover how it speaks to us in our own situations of crisis. The Song evokes an incomparably beautiful land, which is Israel and more than Israel—a land rich with the domestic wealth of wheat and wine, but also with exotic spices, myrrh, and frankincense (3:6). The Song enables us to imagine relating to this land in love—and I suggest two ways that such imagining should inform our prayers, and our lives.

First, pondering that love of the land of Israel, we may deepen our prayers for the peace of the world. The psalmist enjoins us to pray regularly for the peace of Jerusalem (Psalm 122:6). Certainly no generation of Christians has been more aware of the need to do so, nor has any had so much painful data to concretize its prayer. As we formulate our prayers, it is important to remember that the Song remains to the very end a poem of desire rather than of satisfaction. So we may pray that those who share God's love for the land of Israel, especially the Jews and Palestinians who live there, may love it patiently, with unswerving devotion in the absence of exclusive possession. Probably there is no emotional feat more difficult for peoples who know that they belong to the land more fully than it can ever belong to them. Therefore those agonized lovers are in very strong need of our prayers.

Second, expanding our view of a beloved land to include the whole earth, we may recognize that we live on a planet that suffers precisely from our lack of love. Could it be that the greatest value of the Song for our generation is to move us to share in God's own love for this beautiful earth? The Talmud preserves an astonishing saying: Anyone who treats the Song lightly, as a mere drinking song, "forfeits his place in the world to come and will bring evil into the world and *imperil the welfare of all humankind.*"[17] The Talmudic rabbis lived centuries before the recognition of a global ecological crisis. Nonetheless, they sensed that the Song has power to counter the depraved images of self and world that go back far in our history and (as we now see) have brought us to this present crisis.

The Song has power to change us precisely because it is a love poem rather than a piece of rationalistic discourse. It is possible—it may be the one thing most worth praying for— that we may be moved to a far deeper love for the earth than most of us now feel or practice. But if that happens, it will not happen through the discourse of politicians, most of whom are arguing the other way anyhow, or even through the presumably more honest findings of scientific commissions. As Wendell Berry has pointed out, if the environmental movement does not become something more than a public cause, then it will surely be a lost one.[18] Pray, then, that we may achieve in our personal lives some measure of integrity, faithfulness, and wholehearted dedication to our most fundamental responsibilities. Care for the "garden" is the first of those responsibilities (Genesis 2:15). Therefore, the intensely personal style of expression in the Song is precisely the key to its spiritual value. If we open ourselves to it, that love language has the potential to effect in us the kind of radical transformation that the New Testament terms *metanoia,* literally, "change of mind"—that is, repentance.

Notes

1. Mishnah Yadayim 3.5. The word *ketubîm* normally refers to the "Writings," the final section of the Hebrew scriptures, and I have rendered it so here. Some translate "all the Scripture," but the narrower frame of reference is more likely. The contents of Torah and Prophets had long been settled, probably centuries before; and it is only the final section about which the rabbis were debating.

2. Tosefta, Sanhedrin 12.10.

3. See Marvin Pope, *The Song of Songs*, Anchor Bible (Garden City: Doubleday, 1972), 336-341.

4. The Hebrew term "a help" (*'ezer*) does not imply subordination, as does the English term "helper." In fact, the opposite is true; the One most often called "a help" is God (see Exodus 18:4, Deuteronomy 33:7, Psalm 70:6).

5. The line may also be translated, "I am my darling's, and my darling is mine."

6. Here I am thinking of Eliot's poems such as "The Wasteland," "Ash Wednesday," and "Four Quartets."

7. We have no idea who was the poet, woman or man, who created the Song of Songs. I use the feminine pronoun to underscore the prominence of the female voice in the poem, although this might be the fictional creation of a man. In any case, the authorial ascription to Solomon (1:1) cannot be historically accurate. The linguistic evidence suggests that the Song of Songs is one of the latest books in the Hebrew Bible, dating to the fourth or third century B.C.E., six centuries or so after Solomon. Furthermore, Solomon, the husband of many wives, is the butt of the final joke of the poem (8:12). The gist of it is this: Let Solomon have his thousands. This lover would rather have just this one woman, "the only one" (6:9).

8. *Song of Songs Rabbah*, ed. Samson Dunsky (Tel Aviv: Devir, 1980), 5.

9. See Genesis 2:15: "And the LORD God took the human being and set him in the Garden of Eden to work it and watch it."

10. For a fuller study of these connections, see my theological commentary, *Proverbs, Ecclesiastes, and The Song of Songs*, Westminster Bible Commentary (Louisville: Westminster/John Knox Press, 2000).

11. Biblical tradition also designates marriage by the word "covenant" (see Malachi 2:14).

12. To the extent that the Song speaks symbolically of the relationship between God and Israel, it is the woman who seems to represent Israel. This does not mean that every utterance of the woman can be read as an address to God, nor can everything said to the woman be heard as an address to Israel. The Song is not a consistent allegory, such as John Bunyan's *Pilgrim's Progress*. Rather, it is a dream poem, which slips among different levels of meaning and sometimes operates on multiple levels simultaneously.

13. Translation from The New Jewish Publication Society *Tanakh* (Philadelphia: Jewish Publication Society, 1985), hereafter NJPS.

14. The passage has an important place in the Jewish High Holiday liturgy, which suggests that it has long been recognized as a central text for knowing Israel's God.

15. The rare verbal root *ḥmq*, translated here "turn away," occurs only in these two passages in all the Bible.

16. From *'Olat Re'ach*, Rabbi Kook's Hebrew commentary on the Siddur (the Jewish prayer book).

17. Tosephta, Sanhedrin 12.10, compare Sandhedrin 101a (italics mine).

18. Wendell Berry, *A Continuous Harmony: Essays Cultural and Agricultural* (New York: Harcourt Brace Jovanovich, 1972), 72 (paraphrased).

PART THREE

THE ART OF
LIVING WELL

THE SWEET FRUIT of intimacy with God is what the biblical writers of both Testaments call "wisdom." It takes time for the tree of human experience to bear the fruit of wisdom. The experience of one person, no matter how hard-won, is not enough; it takes a tradition, the accumulated experience and insight of a people, to produce wisdom. In these chapters, we will explore the so-called wisdom books—Proverbs, Ecclesiastes, and Job—in which Israel preserved understandings garnered over generations. These books also honor the wisdom of those who challenged accepted understandings and thus pushed the tradition forward into previously uncharted territory. How, for example, does the wise person understand what for all the world looks like the enmity of God? The sages of Israel take us into the realm of religious knowledge that is utterly practical and confirmable by common experience, yet nonetheless not obvious.

CHAPTER EIGHT

WISE IGNORANCE

The Book of Proverbs

PROBABLY FEW PEOPLE would put the book of Proverbs on their shortlist of favorite spiritual books. At first glance, there does not seem to be anything very spiritual or uplifting about it. On the contrary, it stands out among the biblical books just because it is so down-to-earth, so ordinary. In fact, Proverbs barely made it into the canon for precisely that reason. Among the first-century rabbis who made the final decisions about which books would be included in what Christians now call the Old Testament, there were some who failed to see here any evidence of inspiration. After all, they said, they're just proverbs, just common sense.

It was my students who taught me the spiritual value of this book. I began teaching it out of a sense of obligation, as a requisite inclusion in courses on the biblical wisdom literature. I was always in a hurry to get on to what seemed to me the really interesting wisdom books: Ecclesiastes and Job. Yet at the end of term, my students repeatedly said, "I wish we had spent more time with Proverbs." So I gradually increased the amount of time allotted to that most basic book of Israelite wisdom. And thus I came to understand that my

92

students liked Proverbs for the very reason I wanted to minimize it: because it is so ordinary. This is a book for unexceptional people trying to live wisely and faithfully in the generally undramatic circumstances of daily life, on the days when water does not pour forth out of rocks and angels do not come to lunch. The Israelite sages are concerned with the same things we worry about, the things people regularly consult their pastors and friends about: how to avoid bitter domestic quarrels, what to tell your kids about sex and about God, what to do when somebody asks you to lend them money, how to handle your own money and your work life, how to cultivate lasting friendships. In short, the sages whose sayings make up Proverbs are interested in the art of living well—with others, with ourselves, with God.

Proverbs is a book to be digested in small bits. Trying to read Proverbs like an airport novel, skimming for plot, is not just heavy but also pointless work. The medieval monks spoke of "chewing" scripture. They said that each word of the Bible is like a grain of spice: you need to hold it in your mouth until it yields its full savor. That is how Proverbs should be read. For this is a book made up entirely of short poems, most of them only a few words long. In Hebrew, the sayings are generally about the length of a modern haiku. Some are popular sayings that have no single author. Others were doubtless the creations of individual poets, most of whose names are now lost to us. But in either case, many of these sayings are not only helpful but also artful. Better, one might say that they are helpful in part because they *are* artful. Here the analogy of the haiku is useful. These poems are designed for the ear and the memory. You can memorize one in a few minutes and carry it around all day long, savoring it. Again, as with haiku, the words are simple. The scenes they sketch are familiar, and they have to be; there is no space here for explanation. But the wisdom preserved is far from obvious. Indeed, it often challenges our ordinary perceptions of how things really do work in the world, and what it is "practical" to know.

We do not know what schools were like in biblical times, but we might suppose that the sages who finally assembled and edited the book of Proverbs were the senior academicians, the tenured professors in ancient Israel's equivalent of the Ivy League. And Proverbs is something like their curriculum for a life-long learning program. Like good teachers of every age, they set forth at the outset their own goals for their "students"—namely, us. They did this, of course, in the form of a poem, somewhat more extended than most of the poems in the book:

> The proverbs of Solomon, son of David,
>   king of Israel—
> For knowing wisdom and discipline,
> for seeing into words of insight.
> For gaining discipline for success:
> righteousness and justice and equity.
> For giving to the naive astuteness,
> to youth, knowledge and discretion.
> Let the wise hear and learn more,
> for seeing into proverb and figure,
> the words of the wise and their riddles.
> The fear of the LORD is the beginning [or, "the best
>   part"] of knowledge;
> wisdom and discipline, fools despise. (1:1-7)

In order to discover the spiritual value of Proverbs, there are several concepts here that need to be chewed: wisdom and knowledge, discipline, fear of the LORD.

"For knowing wisdom and discipline": the first phrase following the title tells us already that the worldview of this book is fundamentally opposed to the dominant worldview in our society. The very idea of wisdom, as the Bible understands it, challenges the mind-set of our society and the view of knowledge that all of us have to some extent internalized. For us, knowledge is a form of power. The idea that my power depends on what I know and (the crucial corollary) *what someone else does not* is fundamental to our whole professionally and technologically oriented society. The military-industrial complex is erected on the idea that specialized knowledge is the highest form of power. So the mystique of specialized knowledge informs everything from Scotch ads (What is this drinker's favorite magazine?) to spy novels to college promotional materials. We encourage our kids to go to graduate school so they will know more than somebody else does and, God willing, get a decent job.

Of course, this is a very old idea; it was old even in biblical times. Centuries before the Israelite sages, Egyptian and Mesopotamian teachers were telling their students, "Study hard, learn to write; there is a future for a good scribe." And they were right. Mastery of hieroglyphics or cuneiform was the work of years. With hundreds or thousands of signs to be learned, very few people achieved literacy. In those societies, writing was arguably the most powerful form of technology. It was a necessary tool for anyone who wished to communicate anything beyond their immediate sphere. So master-scribes were the "information managers" of their culture. The best of them might rise to the top of the government or temple hierarchy. Consequently, Egyptian and Mesopotamian scribes tried to keep their students in school (and paying tuition!) by composing literature that praised the good life enjoyed by the scribe:

> I have seen how the belabored man is belabored—
> thou should set thy heart in pursuit of writing. And
> I have observed how one may be rescued from his
> duties—behold, there is nothing that surpasses writ-

ing.... I shall make thee love writing more than thy own mother. [1]

There is a pronounced contrast between such scribal literature and what we find in Proverbs. The lure that the Israelite sages offer their students has little or nothing to do with personal professional advancement. Although they speak of "gaining discipline for success," consider how they define success: the establishment of righteousness, justice, and equity. By their reckoning, the one who is wise aims at goodness, not power.

95

That motivation distinguishes Israel's sages, not only from their ancient counterparts, but also from modern academicians, of which I am one. "Righteousness and justice and equity"—I am struck by how weird that rationale for an educational program sounds if I try to set it in the context of virtually any contemporary institution. Scholars who populate universities and seminaries all have a great deal of highly specialized knowledge. They have expertise, but most would think it odd to speak of what they know as tending toward "righteousness." The problem with that claim is not that it is pretentious (pretentiousness is acceptable enough in the academy); rather, it represents a mistake in category assignment. Modern scholars are not hired for righteousness' sake. Our graduate training prepares us to think rigorously, creatively; those are the standards by which we learn to value ourselves and our work. Moreover, this perspective is widely shared even in theological academies. I cannot recall the subject of righteousness ever coming up in any job interview in which I have participated, as interviewer or interviewee. And that in itself shows how far we are from the sages' view of education, because righteousness is *all* they are concerned about. The Bible shows no interest whatsoever in abstract knowledge—that is, in knowledge abstracted from goodness. It is worth noting that ancient Israel seems to have invested little intellectual capital in astronomy, architecture, engineering, medicine, the fine arts—areas in which the neighboring empires of Egypt and Mesopotamia excelled. In sum, Israel was not interested in any form of knowledge that is abstracted from the concrete problem of how we may live in kindness and fidelity with our neighbors, live humbly and faithfully in the presence of God.

The fourth-century theologian Augustine of Hippo helps us understand something about the kind of knowledge that tends toward goodness. He makes a distinction between *sapientia* and *scientia,* terms that may be best rendered in English as "wisdom" and "abstract knowledge." Of *sapientia* Augustine says simply: "True wisdom is such that no evil use can ever be made of it." *Scientia* is not inherently evil; it is problematic only in that abstract knowledge has no intrinsic relationship with goodness. Although the story may be apocryphal, some claim that when Albert Einstein heard about the atomic bombings of Hiroshima and Nagasaki, he commented: "It goes to show that you cannot do whatever you want"—and, one might add, "whatever you know how to do." Inherent to *scientia* is the danger that it can be so easily misdirected to our selfish, short-sighted ends.

But "true wisdom is such that no evil use can ever be made of it." That is worth our pondering because we, more than any previous generation, are witnessing the evil effects of perverted knowledge, knowledge not essentially connected to goodness. We are seeing those effects manifested, probably for the first time in human history, on a global scale. No other generation has been so successful at using its technological knowledge in order to manipulate the world and satisfy its own appetites. The ecological crisis is essentially a crisis of knowledge run amok. Through us, powerful abstract human knowledge (*scientia*) is operating upon the world, changing it in fundamental ways. We are doing, it seems, whatever we know how to do, yet our knowledge is, paradoxically, uninformed.

And what should inform our knowledge? If, as Augustine says, the essence of wisdom is that it is incapable of being directed to harmful ends, then perhaps that is because wisdom takes account of its own ignorance. A sage named Agur, one of the very few Israelite sages whose name is known to us, laments:

97

> I am brutish, less than a man;
> I don't have the insight of a human being! (30:2)

The exclamation is startling, coming almost at the end of the book of Proverbs—after we have (potentially) digested hundreds of wise sayings and should, it seems, be feeling pretty smart. But one must wonder: is Agur merely a typical insecure academic, always aware that there are a lot of folks out there smarter than he is, and afraid of being caught out? Or is he modeling something about what in fact it means to be a wise person? Maybe Agur—or the ancient editors who put his words near the end of Proverbs—was not willing to let us end our reading without understanding that true wisdom is not really the opposite of ignorance. Rather, wisdom and ignorance are two sides of the same coin. Consider this: none of us can anticipate, or even know in retrospect, more than a fraction of the consequences of our actions. So wisdom must mean acting (or refraining from action) in full acknowledgment of our own ignorance. One modern sage, farmer and plant geneticist Wes Jackson, suggests the following principle as the basis for his "agrarian perspective":

> Since our ignorance (about how we are affecting natural systems) far outweighs our knowledge, let's go with our strong suit and develop an ignorance-based economy.[2]

Wisdom, then, has an inherent modesty. It does not manipulate the world based on a set of abstract principles that are supposed to be valid because they are "scientific." Rather, the wise enter into contemplative relationship with the world: they watch before they act upon the world. Often they watch for a long time. They are looking to see what God has done. Because they take the time to grow in love and respect—the qualities of all healthy relationships—their actions are less likely to be harmful. In recent generations we humans have greatly increased our technical ability, but our wisdom has not grown in like measure. In Augustine's terms, *scientia* has vastly outpaced *sapientia*. In the present situation, survival—for our own species and for others—may well depend on *homo sapiens* forswearing the promiscuous use of our minds in the undisciplined search for knowledge.

Three Alien Concepts: Discipline, Obedience, Fear
The concept of discipline is fundamental to what the sages would have us learn. In their vocabulary, the term is frequently paired with wisdom, and both are wholly positive. But this also marks a difference between their educational perspective and our own. For us, discipline is a largely negative concept. The word does not even appear in some contemporary translations of Proverbs.[3] "Discipline" sounds antiquated and distinctly unpleasant; it evokes images of detention halls and nuns rapping knuckles with rulers. But the sages view the matter in quite another way, as their saying shows:

> One who loves discipline loves knowledge;
> and one who hates reproof is brutish. (12:1)

Proverbs is not addressed to people with fragile egos. One of the stock characters in Proverbs is the fool. A fool is someone who refuses correction or reproof because she cannot

seriously entertain the possibility of being wrong. The wise
person, on the other hand, actively seeks out discipline,
which is never wholly comfortable; but no pain, no gain. A
remarkable saying implies that discipline is the most basic
form of self-regard:

99

> The one who breaks loose from discipline rejects
>   his own self,
> but one who hears reproof acquires a heart.
> The fear of the LORD is discipline, wisdom;
> and before glory, meekness. (15:32-33)

What sort of self is it that the sages envision, that we
reject when we "break loose from discipline"? The sages sub-
scribe to a dynamic notion of human personhood. The
"self" of which they speak is not a static entity, a fixed identity and destiny given at birth. Rather, through discipline,
one "*acquires* a heart," as the Tin Woodman hoped to do. In
the metaphorical physiology of the Bible, the heart is the
organ of cognition and faith as well as of emotion. It is the
thinking, feeling, believing center of the person who is coming into full being before God. Thus the sages see selfhood as
something that necessarily develops over time. Shrewd pastoral psychologists that they are, they know that if discipline
is not continually cultivated, then the emerging self erodes.

If the sages rejected the static view of the human person
held by some of their contemporaries, they would equally
reject the "ultra-dynamic" view of personhood that is popular in postmodern culture—that is, the belief that we essentially invent (and reinvent) ourselves. The Israelite sages
would view as a sad delusion our contemporary "faith" that
we craft an identity out of a certain constellation of tastes
and ambitions, as well as clothing, cars, houses, domestic
partners, and other props; that all these presumed elements

of the self are infinitely manipulable, and a new "self" can be assembled at will, or at whim.

In contrast to both these notions, the Israelite sages understood that one gains a truly human heart by receiving guidance and accepting correction from others who know us, in a sense, better than we can know ourselves. But how can they know us that well? Because they know God, in whose image we are made. That is why human selfhood is not static: because God is a living God. And because we are made in God's image, we are not "making ourselves up" as we go along. A stable self develops through one means only: the difficult discipline of obedience to those who are ahead of us in our journey toward God.

Like discipline, obedience has been devalued as an educational concept in our culture; we relegate it to the realm of animal training. Yet obedience is quite literally the starting point of the sages' curriculum. The very first word following the opening poem is *shema'*: "hear, obey."

> *Shema'* my child, the discipline of your father,
> and do not forsake the teaching (*tôrah*) of your
>   mother. (1:8)

The first word arrests attention, for it is the first word of what has long been regarded by Jews as the most important statement in the Bible:

> *Shema' Yisra'el*, hear, O Israel, the LORD your God is
> one LORD; and you shall love the LORD your God with
> all your heart and with all your self and with all your
> power. (Deuteronomy 6:4-5)

The sages here boldly put the instruction of mother and father under the sacred rubric of Torah, the term applied to the great teaching of Moses from Sinai, which Israel must obey in order to live (Deuteronomy 30:15).

In English as in Hebrew, the word "obedience" denotes acute listening. Our English word derives from the Latin root *audio:* "hear, listen." *Ob-audio* means literally "listen toward"; the preposition *ob-* begets an image of someone bending forward to catch every word of a revered speaker, eager to receive direction—even correction. In the Christian tradition, it is the monastics who can teach us most about the exacting discipline of obedience. They teach out of hard experience. Any honest monastic will admit that the "obedience" vow is the hardest. One gets used to poverty and chastity—those may even be a relief. But for most, obedience remains difficult, and it must be so; for obedience is the anvil on which the Christian self is being forged, shaped, and sometimes hammered into a thing of strength and beauty. So the great monastic theologian Augustine set forth for the monks the truth that is not obvious, that obedience to their superior is an act of kindness to themselves.[4]

The core idea of the monastic life is the same one the sages set forth here: the inner self is made firm, paradoxically enough, through allowing the good judgment of another to override one's own will. That idea holds good for those of us who are not under formal vows of obedience as well. We grow as Christians by listening acutely to others, living and dead, within the community of faith, and letting their authority be a shaping force in our lives. That is what it means to stand within a tradition. I am not sure we acknowledge sufficiently how much trust such acceptance requires. That is why obedience is especially difficult for us, because trust is in short supply in our society and in our church. We speak often of "healthy suspicion"; in contemporary academic circles, suspicion has even been elevated to the status of a "hermeneutic," a basic principle of interpretation. Suspicion can be healthy and is often necessary for correcting the system. But the insight of the sages is that spiritual growth requires trust above all. Their advice to us is this: find someone further along than you, a mother or father in faith. And when you find someone whose guidance you can accept for at least this stage of your journey toward God—then lean forward, listen acutely, obey.

"The fear of the LORD is discipline, wisdom" (15:33)—here the sages introduce a third concept that is indispensable for them, and difficult for us. The sages of Proverbs do not hesitate to equate "fear of the LORD" with wisdom itself. From the outset they advise:

> The fear of the LORD is the beginning (or "the best part") of knowledge;
> wisdom and discipline, fools despise. (1:7)

This verse, or a variation on it, is repeated over and over. Consistently, Proverbs upholds "fear" as a healthy and necessary disposition toward God. That in itself is to modern readers one of the most offensive things in the Old Testament. Aware of this offense, many recent translations of the Bible speak instead of "reverence for God"—a phrase that has less evident neurotic content. That rendering is not exactly wrong; certainly reverence is part of what the sages mean to commend to us. Yet in avoiding the word "fear," translators are taking the edge off the point that the biblical writers are making. The writers are speaking first of all of our proper gut response to God. Fear is an elemental response; reverence is a head trip. Fear is the unmistakable feeling in our bodies, in our stomachs and our scalp, when we run up hard against the power of God.

From a biblical perspective, there is nothing neurotic about fearing God. The neurotic thing is *not* to be afraid, or to be afraid of the wrong thing. That is why God chooses to be known to us, so that we may stop being afraid of the wrong thing. When God is fully revealed to us and we "get it," then we experience the conversion of our fear. Probably the most striking biblical witness to this conversion is the account of the crossing of the Red Sea. On the western shore, Israel looked up, and "here is Egypt coming after them, and they were really afraid" (Exodus 14:10). And then, on the far shore, Israel looked again, and this time it saw "Egypt dead, on the edge of the Sea. And Israel saw what the great hand of the LORD had done against Egypt, and the people feared the LORD..." (Exodus 14:31).

103

The time comes in every life—and more than once—when we are personally confronted with the power that spread out the heavens like a sequined veil, that formed us out of dust and blew breath into our lungs, that led Israel through the Red Sea on dry land and left Pharaoh's whole army floating behind. If we can experience that power close up and *not* be gripped in our guts by the disparity between God and ourselves, then we are in a profound state of spiritual slumber, if not acute mental illness. "Fear of the LORD" is the deeply sane recognition that we are not God.

Notes

1. "The Satire on the Trades" (Egyptian, Middle Kingdom), in James B. Prichard, ed., *Ancient Near Eastern Texts Relating to the Old Testament* (Princeton: Princeton University Press, 1978), 432.

2. Personal communication. On the agrarian perspective, see Wes Jackson, *Becoming Native to This Place* (Lexington: University Press of Kentucky, 1994), and also the final chapter in this book.

3. The NRSV incorrectly renders the word as "instruction" in Proverbs 1:2 and 1:3.

4. The Rule of St. Augustine, II:7.

CHAPTER NINE

SIMPLE GIFTS

The Book of Ecclesiastes

THE BOOK OF PROVERBS represents what might be called "mainstream" Israelite wisdom—which is not to say predictable, or lacking in insight. On the contrary, the sayings that appear in Proverbs are often profound and even at times surprising, yet they never shock the pious. But now, turning to the book of Ecclesiastes, we encounter the teachings of the most eccentric of the sages, known to his contemporaries by the wholly unique name of Kohelet. It is less a name than a job description: it means something like "one who gathers an assembly." Maybe this name is itself the first of many subtly ironic statements in the book, for one has the sense that people must always have walked away from a session with Kohelet shaking their heads, no longer certain just what to believe.

This book has been regarded from the beginning, it seems, as a biblical anomaly. As with Proverbs, the first-century rabbis who made the final decisions about what books would be included in the canon debated its inclusion, and ever since there have been those who deny that it has any revelatory value. Yet Martin Luther believed that Christians should read "this noble little book" on a daily basis, and a Vietnam War chaplain attested that this was the one part of the Bible his soldiers were willing to hear. One of my former students, who suffers from recurrent bouts of depression, says that reading Ecclesiastes is for her "like slipping into a warm bath." She feels soothed, supported; her perception of reality has been articulated within the pages of scripture. She is not crazy, no longer alone.

So who was this Kohelet, and what can he tell us about the good life? The first words of the book imply that he is to be identified with Solomon, "the son of David, king in Jerusalem" (1:1). But the linguistic evidence suggests this ascription is a literary fiction. The language here is close to Hebrew of the rabbinic period. This is probably one of the latest books in the Old Testament, written centuries after Solomon—most likely in the first half of the third century B.C.E., when Jerusalem had become a sophisticated Hellenistic city. The words of Kohelet seem to have been originally addressed to young men with "good prospects," Jews who had assimilated well enough to Greek culture to know some philosophy[1] and who were expected to make a place for themselves in business, or perhaps as minor court officials or magistrates. It is interesting that among all the sages, Kohelet is the only one specifically described in an active teaching role:

Not only was Kohelet a wise man,
he also taught knowledge to the people,
weighing and studying and arranging
    many proverbs. (12:9)

Maybe he was an instructor at the ancient equivalent of a Jerusalem prep school, where his students were the sons of the well-to-do, the next generation of "movers and shakers."

Kohelet's strategy with his students is to beat them at their own game—which is to say, he outdoes his students in the skepticism characteristic of youth:

"Vanity of vanities," said Kohelet,
"vanity of vanities, all is vanity. . . .
All things are wearisome—
one cannot express it.
The eye is unsatisfied with seeing,
and the ear does not get filled from listening.
What has been, that is what will be;
and what has been done, that is what will be done.
There is nothing at all new under the sun.
There is a phenomenon of which someone says,
'See this, it's new!'
It has already been for ages,
those that were before us.
There is no remembrance for former generations,
nor will there be for generations to come.
They will have no remembrance
among those who come after them." (1:2, 8-11)

No contemporary adolescent could be more scathing in describing the delusions under which her successful and success-driven parents labor. For this reason, the book retains to this day a special appeal for youth of high school and college age, as well as for young adults struggling with the disappointments of "the real world." One by one, Kohelet exposes the absurdity of our pretensions to uniqueness, our expectations of lasting fame or enduring achievement. Just because the challenge to our common delusions is so radical, his identity becomes important. Perhaps this explains why the book is ascribed to Solomon. Any lesser figure who dismissed the ultimate value of human wisdom, achievement, and wealth would be open to the charge of sour grapes. The early rabbis took the Solomonic ascription at face value. Otherwise, they remark, "people might say, 'This fellow, who never owned two cents, presumes to despise all the good things of the world!'"[2] But as it is, Kohelet's words come to us with the authority of someone rich, worldly, and wise, who renders this comprehensive judgment from experience:

> I applied myself to inquire and investigate wisely concerning everything that is done under the heavens. It is a bad business that God has given to human beings to be busy with! I saw all the deeds that are done under the sun, and look! It is all vanity and chasing after wind. (1:13-14)

Kohelet's radical nay-saying is a shock to the pious. Yet he is no mere cynic, content to strip us of illusions and then leave us comfortless. Rather, his nay-saying is the means by which this teacher instructs us in a matter essential to the life of faith. From the mainstream sages of Proverbs we may learn about the nature of "righteousness, justice, and equity" (Proverbs 1:3), but Kohelet teaches us about humility. This is the core of his teaching: life can never be mastered, if "mastery" means shaping it in conformity with our desires. It can only be enjoyed, when pleasures great and small come our way. Or, when enjoyment is not possible, then life must be endured. What Kohelet aims to instill in his students is the ability to receive the pleasures of life as the gift they are and to recognize God as sole Giver—"For who eats or who feels anything, apart from him?" (2:25).

It is often said that the message of Ecclesiastes is best summed up as *carpe diem*, "seize the day." But the evidence belies that. The key verb in the book is not "seize" but "give," which occurs twenty-eight times in these twelve chapters— and most often the one who gives is God. The essential message, then, is "Receive the gift." We practice the core religious virtue of humility by noting with pleasure, day by day, the gifts that come to us from God. And the truth is, most of those are given so regularly that we never even pause to recognize them for the gifts they are.

> Sweet is the light, and good for the eyes
> it is to see the sun. (11:7)

For Jerusalemites, sunny days are more the rule than the exception. This is a small poem (seventeen syllables in Hebrew—exactly the length of a Japanese haiku) about the most ordinary of phenomena: the sunlight that shines on the just and the unjust alike. The fact that Kohelet's brief teaching takes the form of a poem is not negligible. In a tone that is far removed from the teacher's lecture or the preacher's harangue, he invites his students to notice just "how sweet it is." The word "sweet" may be overused in our language, but the equivalent adjective (*matôk*) is rare in biblical Hebrew. So when Kohelet, the consummate nay-sayer, uses that word of simple appreciation, we should take notice. Thus he seeks to initiate us into the daily, down-to-earth practice of humility, the blessed disposition that Jesus himself called "poverty of spirit" (Matthew 5:3).

The word "humility" derives from the Latin word *humus,* meaning "soil." Ecclesiastes is a thoroughly earth-bound book whose focus is on human prospects "under the sun." Kohelet refuses to speculate on the heavenly realm:

> For God is in the heavens and you upon the earth,
> therefore let your words be few. (5:1)

Nor does Kohelet hope for an afterlife. He rejects the possibility of immortality with a firmness that some find offensive:

> I thought, I, within my own heart-and-mind, concerning human beings, to dissociate them from divinity,

and to see that animals is what they really are.[3] For what happens to human beings, that is the same thing that happens to animals. As is the death of the one, so is the death of the other; and there is one breath belonging to all. And the advantage of human beings over animals—it is non-existent! For everything is fleeting [traditionally: "vanity"].[4] Everything goes to one place.

Everything was from the dust,
and everything returns to the dust.

Who knows that the breath of human beings rises upward, and the breath of animals descends below, to the earth? Indeed, I have seen that there is nothing better than that a person should take joy in his doings, for that is his portion. For who can bring him to see what will be after him? (3:18-22)

Obviously, Kohelet's religious vision falls short of the full promise of the gospel. Early Judaism—including the Jew Jesus and his first followers—turned decisively away from Kohelet's utter lack of expectation for life after death. So to this day, orthodox Jews along with Christians affirm their faith in the resurrection of the dead. But despite that one departure from Kohelet's thinking, both faith communities accept his book as authoritative and thus uphold his core teaching on accepting and cherishing the gifts of God.

"There is nothing better than that a person should take joy in his doings" (3:22). Always Kohelet is on the look-out for the possibility of joy. But vague encouragement—"Have a good day!"—is not enough for him. He specifically urges us to realize three forms of happiness in our lives: sensual pleasure (eating and drinking, sleep, sunlight), intimate relationships (friendship and conjugal love), and satisfaction in work. Further, his insistence on enjoyment is something completely different from advocating hedonism. Finding joy in life is a genuinely religious form of humility. Because it is God "who makes all [or 'everything']" (11:5), ultimately God is the Author of every form of enjoyment. The fact that Kohelet breeds in his students love of the world, rather than fear or contempt, is another reason for his enduring appeal to the young.

Joy and Ephemerality

The great problem in making sense of Ecclesiastes is how to reconcile these two things that seem to be mutually exclusive: on the one hand, Kohelet's insistence on enjoyment, and on the other, the pronouncement that stands over the whole book, *havel havalîm*—traditionally translated "vanity of vanities." However, "vanity" is only an approximate translation of the Hebrew word *hevel*.[5] One modern commentator renders it "absurdity."[6] Kohelet is struck and appalled by the total disparity between what *should* happen in a well-ordered world and what actually *does* happen. Far more than earlier sages, Kohelet acknowledges that the phenomenon of moral disorder and contradiction is an enduring reality with which the religious person must wrestle. Here he gives one instance of such moral absurdity:

> There is *hevel* that is done on the earth, namely
> there are righteous people, and what comes to them
>   is what fits the doing of the wicked;
> and there are wicked people, and what comes to
>   them is what fits the doing of the righteous.
> I said that this, too, is *hevel*. (8:14)

But "absurdity" is not all that *hevel* suggests. The literal meaning of the word is "a mist, vapor, breath." At times, what Kohelet calls *hevel* is something fragile and ephemeral that disappears without trace. The hard fact of human mortality moves him to render this comprehensive judgment:

> And the advantage of human beings over animals—it is non-existent! For everything is *hevel*.
>
> Everything goes to one place.
> Everything was from the dust,
> and everything returns to the dust. (3:19-20)

In the face of death, everyone and everything is *hevel*, evaporating like early morning mist beneath the strong Jerusalem sun.

Absurdity and ephemerality—these two aspects of *hevel* ultimately work together. Martin Luther, who shows a lively appreciation of Ecclesiastes unmatched in the Christian tradition, remarks incisively that the very fact that life passes quickly away exposes the absurdity of some of our most common behaviors. What Kohelet condemns is

> the depraved affection and desire of us people, who are not content with the creatures [created things] of God that we have and with their use but are always anxious and concerned to accumulate riches, honors, glory, and fame, as though we were going to live here forever; and meanwhile we become bored with the things that are present and continually yearn for other things, and then still others. . . . This is really being suspended between heaven and earth![7]

Kohelet may have had in mind yet a third association of this word *hevel*. The word appears once in the Bible as the name of an individual. It is the Hebrew spelling of the name Abel. Abel's name is his history: ephemerality, absurdity. He enters the biblical story only to die young and senselessly. Kohelet has meditated long and hard on the first few chapters of Genesis, and he echoes its message of our inescapable mortality: "Everything returns to the dust." In light of Kohelet's preoccupation with death, it is quite possible to hear his initial comprehensive pronouncement—"everyone (or everything) is *hevel*"—as identifying us, every one of us, with Abel (Hevel), son of Adam, the first human being to die. Kohelet does not try to persuade us of the sentimental and ultimately cruel view that every death—or any death—makes sense. Rather, invoking Abel, he reminds us that death is at every moment a possibility for all of us, and therefore he would not have us live foolishly or die "suddenly and unprepared."[8]

The reality of death conditions every moment of life. Kohelet never lets us forget that our days "under the sun" are flying past and will soon be done. But he expects us to be cheerful despite that knowledge—indeed, more cheerful *because of it:*

> Go, eat with pleasure your bread
> and drink with a happy heart your wine,
> for already God has approved your doings.
> In every season let your clothes be white
> and let not oil be lacking upon your head,
> Enjoy life with the woman you love,
> all the days of your fleeting life [*hevel*-life]
> which God has given you under the sun—all your
>   fleeting days—
> for that is your portion in life and in your toil
> with which you are toiling under the sun. (9:7-9)

For all his debunking, Kohelet never dismisses joy itself as *hevel*—an absurdity, mere ephemerality. Rather, joy and *hevel* are complementary. Joy is the one thing strong enough to stand up in the face of all that is disappointing, in the face of the fact that all we do achieve and value is passing away and will surely be forgotten. Recognizing that, we might well succumb to ennui or despair. But Kohelet says, No, rejoice, even in the face of death itself. Maybe it is the shadow of death itself that enables us to invest ourselves so deeply in this imperfect life, these imperfect people "under the sun":

> Whatever your hand finds to do, do it with all
>   your might,
> for there is no doing or thought or knowledge or
>   wisdom in Sheol,
> to which you are going. (9:10)

One of many seeming contradictions in this book is that Kohelet completely rejects the notion of any lasting human achievements, yet he tells us to do whatever we do with everything we've got. Moreover, he offers the stunning assurance, unparalleled in the Bible, that "already God has approved your doings" (9:7). This might be a dangerous assurance if it were addressed to an audience of potential arsonists. But Kohelet is not talking to those who have cast off all restraint. Much more likely, he is speaking to people like us: extremely responsible, moderately religious folk who are perpetually anxious to do the right thing. Kohelet understands them because he is one of them: those who strive for great achievements and try to make sense of everything, to secure the future against disaster and the system against injustice—and because they can never wholly succeed, they are in grave danger, as Kohelet says of himself, of "hat[ing] life, for grievous to me is the doing that is done under the sun—for everything is *hevel* and chasing after wind" (2:17).

To the perpetually anxious, Kohelet offers the healthful asceticism of letting go of our vain pretense to determine the future and instead focusing resolutely on the present, receiving with an open hand the pleasures and the opportunities it offers. Among them is the opportunity to work hard—and sometimes, by the gift of God, to derive pleasure from the work we do. This is perhaps the area where Kohelet can be most helpful to modern westerners, for he reflects more carefully on the nature of work than does any other biblical writer. Therefore he can help us with our own pressing need to develop a sane theology of work. For we are, on the whole, a people who work very hard and get too little pleasure from our work. Kohelet could be speaking directly to us:

> This is what I myself have seen to be good, yes, beautiful: to eat and drink and take pleasure in all the toil with which one toils under the sun the number of days of life which God has given one.... [T]o accept one's lot and to rejoice in one's toil—this, it is the gift of God. (5:17-18)

Kohelet is not idealistic about work. Hard work is a necessity, and the gift of joy that may come from it can only be received; it cannot be coerced. Moreover, Kohelet harbors no illusions about why most of us work as hard as we do: we do it to beat out the competition. "I myself have seen all the toil and the skill in doing, that it is envy, one person of another. This, too, is *hevel* and chasing after wind" (4:4). We do not know any work that is not affected, you might say, by our fallen condition; pride and jealousy are powerful motivating factors for excellence. Yet insofar as we strive to best our neighbor, to that extent we are chasing after wind.

"Chasing after wind"—the Hebrew phrase may convey a sense that is not obvious in translation. As is well known, the Hebrew word *ruah* means "wind," but also "spirit"; so it is possible to see some deflating of our spiritual pretensions here. Work is for many people a matter of "chasing after spirit." Probably this is more true in our society than it was in the ancient world, so Kohelet himself may not intend a pun. But I do see here a play on meanings that reflects our modern context. This is our own peculiar form of *hevel*, absurdity: we overwork, looking not for pleasure, which work can give, but for something it cannot, something that we vaguely term "spiritual satisfaction." Professional commitment is one of the primary forms of idolatry among white-collar Amer-icans—and here I include clergy collars. Looking for ultimate meaning in any form of work, including church work, inevitably leads to deep disappointment and bitterness. When one does not get the desired promotion; when one's own vision for the program, the institution, the community does not prevail; or perhaps when one just burns out from too much effort expended, too little pleasure received as a gift from God—all this is *hevel* and chasing after wind.

Learning to Lose Ourselves
Kohelet is often wrongly viewed as a cynic. Whereas a cynic is someone who has settled, more or less comfortably, into a fixed view of life (a negative one), Kohelet is a lifelong learner, a true wise man. The best evidence for this is the fact that at the end of his book, we see a very different perspective on life than the one with which he began. The haunting poem in the final chapter is generally called "the allegory of death":

> Remember your Creator, in the days of your youth,
> before the evil days come,
> and the years arrive when you will say, "I have no
> delight in them."...
> On the day when the guards of the house shake,
> and the strong men tremble,
> and the grinding women cease, for they are few
> and the women who look out through the windows
> are darkened. (12:1, 3)

These several metaphors for "the evil days" are commonly taken as referring to the disabilities of old age: tottering limbs, teeth that can no longer chew, eyes grown dim.

116

> and the dust returns to the earth as it was,
> and the breath (or "spirit")⁹ returns to God who
> gave it.
> "*Havel havalîm,*" said Kohelet,
> "Everything is *hevel.*" (12:7-8)

The poems that begin and end the book are a matched pair, in that they have the same refrain: "*Havel havalîm,* absurdity of absurdities, ephemerality of ephemeralities." Yet what strikes me is how different in tone the two poems are. At the beginning of the book, Kohelet is world-weary, jaded, as he laments the pointlessness of it all: "There is nothing at all new under the sun.... There is no remembrance for former generations, nor will there be for generations to come" (1:9, 11). By the end of the book, the facts have not changed, but Kohelet's response is dramatically altered. Now he speaks with open urgency: "Remember!"—though we ourselves will be forgotten. Although nothing is really new, still every season of life is not the same. Youth is the time for remembering your Creator, "before the evil days come" (12:1). There is something of Dylan Thomas's tone here, in the poem written for his dying father: "Do not go gentle into that good night." But there is also a difference. Thomas urges, "Rage, rage against the dying of the light."¹⁰ Kohelet says, "Remember your Creator." It is the difference between furiously grasping at your ebbing life, and recollecting in calmness and sobriety both life's source and its fleeting quality.

"Remember your Creator, *in the days of your youth.*" There will come a time for many of us when we will need all our strength just to endure, when memory and judgment will no longer be reliable. There may come a time when even repentance is no longer possible. It is a sobering thought, that someday we may lack the flexibility of mind and spirit to turn back to God. Kohelet does not pull his punches: bearing gracefully the losses that attend old age requires more than courage; we must also grow wise. "Remember your Creator—and do it now," he tells his youthful students. Kohelet's profound insight is that a good old age (to say nothing of a good death) takes years of preparation, years of "un-selfing." We do well to start young, getting unstuck from a fixation on our own egos, our own accomplishments and desires, even our own best qualities.

117

In the course of his book, Kohelet takes us through the whole journey from preoccupation with self to a costly forgetfulness of self. This is evident even in his language. In the opening chapters, Kohelet uses the first person pronoun over and over. That usage is a striking mark of his style, because pronouns are unnecessary in most Hebrew sentences. Since all verbs are inflected (internally marked for person, number, and gender), pronouns are generally used only for emphasis. But at the outset, Kohelet repeatedly uses the pronoun *'anî*, "I." Thus he calls attention to his own viewpoint and action:

I, Kohelet, I was king over Israel in Jerusalem. (1:12)

I said, I, to my heart, Look, I, I have grown great and accumulated wisdom. (1:16)

I said, I, in my heart, Come on, let me conduct an experiment in enjoyment. (2:1)

Yet by the end of the book, when he gives "the end of the matter," he has moved 180 degrees:

God you shall fear, and his commandments keep; for this is every person. (12:13)

Some scholars regard this as a pious addition by some meddling editor, but consider another possibility: could this not be the authentic voice of the wise teacher who has seen it all, done it all, and come up with no new sources of meaning for human life? Rather than being a pious platitude, it can be taken as a statement of utter humility. In a poem that owes much to Kohelet, the modern Christian poet T. S. Eliot says:

The only wisdom we can hope to acquire
Is the wisdom of humility: humility is endless.[11]

Kohelet takes the grand tour of life, and in the end his sophistication gains him no wisdom more valuable than what he first learned as a child at home. It is no different from the traditional wisdom his mother might have taught him, straight out of Torah and Proverbs: "Fear God and keep his commandments." But the final phrase is Kohelet's signature: "For this is every person." Translating more literally, one could read: "This is every Adam—every human being." It is a startling statement, so much so that translators habitually try to domesticate it, as in the *New Revised Standard Version*: "For that is the whole duty of everyone." But Kohelet's summary is in fact far more radical. Fearing God and keeping the commandments is more than a duty. It is what constitutes our humanity. It is our personhood. Kohelet is a man who has owned up fully to disillusionment and despair; he has looked unblinkingly at old age and death. Having done so, he is sobered but fearless—or almost so. Only one fear is left, and Kohelet more than any other biblical writer shows us what fear of God looks like "under the sun." It is a posture of complete humility—that is, groundedness—and openhanded receptivity.

Learning to receive life as pure gift, we gradually prepare ourselves to receive even God. The medieval Christian mystic

Meister Eckhart has a teaching that might serve as a commentary on Ecclesiastes:

> God does not give gifts, nor did he ever give one, so
> that people might keep it and take satisfaction in it;
> but all were given—all he ever gave on earth or in
> heaven—that he might give this one more: himself. Therefore I say that we must learn to look
> through every gift and every event to God and never
> be content with the thing itself. There is no stopping
> place in this life—no, nor was there ever for any person, no matter how far along one's way one had gone.
> This above all, then, be ready for the gifts of God and
> always for new ones.[12]

119

From this we can begin to understand why some
Christians, including profound theologians such as Jerome
and Luther, have seen this resolutely earth-bound book of
Ecclesiastes as preparing the way for Christ. Theirs is a fairly
obvious argument: by his relentless debunking, Kohelet
weans us from all false wisdom and thus prepares the way for
Jesus Christ, the true wisdom of God (1 Corinthians 1:24).
Less obvious, but perhaps more penetrating, is the insight
that Kohelet aims chiefly to enable us to receive the gifts of
God—and Christians understand that Christ is the ultimate
gift. There is "a season for every matter under the heavens"
(3:1), and perhaps the liturgical season best suited to
Kohelet's book is Advent. Ecclesiastes does not prepare us for
Christ's coming as does Isaiah, by prophetic promises and
messianic visions. Yet in a quite different way this book suits
the mood of that sober-but-not-grim season, when we seek
to open our hearts to receive the ever-new gift of God in
Christ.

Notes

1. There are clear points of connection between ideas Kohelet articulates and contemporary Greek philosophy. See the fuller discussion in my commentary, *Proverbs, Ecclesiastes, and the Song of Songs*, Westminster Bible Companion (Louisville: Westminster/ John Knox Press, 2000).

2. *Midrash Kohelet Rabba* 3:11, cited in *Koheleth—The Man and His World, a Study of Ecclesiastes* (New York: Schocken Books, 1968), 40.

3. The meaning of 3:18 is highly uncertain, and the text may be corrupt. My translation follows (approximately) the NJPS *Tanakh*.

4. The Hebrew word here translated as "fleeting" is *hevel*. See the discussion of this word in the following section.

5. The vowels are variable in Hebrew words; the constant letters by which the root is recognized are the consonants *h-v-l*.

6. Michael V. Fox, *Qohelet and His Contradictions* (Sheffield: Sheffield Academic Press, 1989).

7. Martin Luther, *Works* (Saint Louis: Concordia Publishing House, 1955–1986) vol. 15, pp. 8, 11.

8. The Great Litany (BCP 149).

9. The Hebrew word is *ruah*, which, as discussed above, means "wind" or "spirit," and also "breath."

10. Dylan Thomas, *Collected Poems 1934-1952* (London: J. M. Dent & Sons, 1952), 116.

11. *Four Quartets*, "East Coker II."

12. "The Talks of Instruction," *Meister Eckhart: A Modern Translation*, trans. Raymond Bernard Blakney (New York: Harper & Row, 1941), 32; translation slightly modified.

CHAPTER TEN

THE SUFFERER'S WISDOM

The Book of Job

IT IS SAFE TO SAY that at the present time the church makes little use of the book of Job for its pastoral ministry. This has not always been the case. The medieval church made heavy use of it in preparing Christian souls to deal with suffering without falling away from their faith. But the modern church has pulled back, even in recent decades. Episcopalians may discover a sign of our retreat in the latest revision of *The Book of Common Prayer* (1979). The Burial Office retains that luminous affirmation: "I know that my Redeemer liveth" (Job 19:25). But gone is Job's statement of resigned grief: "The LORD gave, and the LORD hath taken away; blessed be the name of the LORD" (1:21). "The LORD hath taken away"—does that in fact express resignation, or is it the beginning of an accusation? That troublingly ambiguous statement is in the 1928 version of *The Book of Common Prayer,* but the 1979 revision pitched it out. And one must ask, Why? Have we grown afraid to lodge the responsibility for our grief with the Lord, as Job so consistently does?

I suspect that we do not more often appeal to the book of Job in times of distress because we do not really know how to read it for the sake of our souls. And in this, modern biblical scholars have not been of great help. Too often they will tell you that what is at stake in this book is the theological question for which the technical term is "theodicy"—in plain language, the question of whether or not God is just. But in fact that question, while present in the book, proves to be a red herring, and Job's hapless counselors get lost following the scent. The focal point of the book is not God's justice at all, but rather the problem of human pain: how Job endures it, cries out of it, wrestles furiously with God in the midst of it, and ultimately transcends his pain—or better, is transformed through it.

The book of Job is about human pain; it is also about theology, the work of speaking about God. In the last chapter, God takes the friends to task, saying, "You have not spoken accurately about me, as has my servant Job" (42:7). Here God is pointing obliquely to what is so remarkable about this book. It shows us a person in the sharpest imaginable pain, yet speaking accurately about God. Job gives us immeasurably more than a theology of *suffering*. It gives us the theology of *a sufferer*. In it we hear authoritative speech about God that comes from lips taut with anguish. From this book above all others in scripture we learn that the person in pain is a theologian of unique authority. The sufferer who keeps looking for God has, in the end, privileged knowledge. The one who complains to God, pleads with God, rails at God, does not let God off the hook for a minute—she is at last admitted to a mystery. She passes through a door that only pain will open, and is thus qualified to speak of God in a way that others, whom we generally call more fortunate, cannot speak.

Does this book teach us sympathy for the sufferer? I don't know. Surely it means to breed in us humility before the one who is suffering. Job instructs us perhaps more about respect than about compassion; if we read this book well, then it enables us to honor the sufferer as a teacher, a theological resource for the community.

Unanswered Questions, Brooding Silences:
The Prologue (Chapters 1-2)
Often good teaching proceeds from leading questions, questions that touch sensitive points and goad us deeper into a subject. Just such questions generate the story of Job. The first two chapters pose a series of highly consequential questions. After all, the whole thing begins with God's proud and naive question to the Satan, who has just returned from an inspection tour of the earth: "Did you notice my servant Job, that there is no one like him on earth, a man of integrity, and straightforward, who fears God and turns from evil?" (1:8).

Likewise, the Satan's cynical reply to God's question is itself a question: "Is it for no good reason that Job fears God?" (1:9). That question is hardly classically diabolical. The Satan as represented here is not a red devil with a pitchfork, tempting poor souls to evil. Rather, he is a member in good standing of the heavenly council, one of God's trusted, if somewhat surly, subordinates. "The Satan" is not a name at all, but rather his job title; we might translate the Hebrew term as "the Adversary." He is something like the chief prosecutor in the divine realm, or the head of the heavenly FBI—not an appealing figure, of course, but that is precisely his role, to prevent any dangerous sentimentality from eroding cosmic order. And that includes any dangerous sentimentality on God's part. So the Satan's questions to God are brilliantly engineered to eradicate romantic delusion from the Divine Lover's heart. "Is it for no good reason that Job fears

God? Haven't you thrown up a protective wall around him and around his house and around everything he has? But now just send forth your hand and touch everything he has—see if he won't curse you to your face!" (1:9-11).

The standoff between God and his professional Adversary looks just like a pagan folktale, where the gods vie for power and prestige, and humanity is inevitably the pawn in the game. By contrast, biblical religion is generally insistent that God does not play dice with the universe. It is shocking, therefore, to see Israel's God accept the dare and, by his own admission, "swallow up [Job] for no good reason" (2:3). If we take that admission at face value, then God looks considerably worse than the Adversary. Maybe the Satan is upholding some notion of cosmic order and fairness. But God appears to be the most vicious kind of stooge, for his cruelty is incidental and therefore utterly indefensible. So we have to ask: Can that face-value reading of the folktale possibly be right, since it invalidates the way God is portrayed everywhere else in the Bible? Unless we are content to imagine that the author of this book does not care at all about what the rest of the Bible says about God—and I am *not* content to imagine that—then we must stop at the outset and try to make sense of this bizarre scene where God accepts the Satan's dare, with its terrible consequences.

The obvious implication of the Satan's questions is that Job has good reason for serving God: he does it for what he gets out of it. In other words, not even God's favorite servant is motivated by love. Now we can see why God has to bite—the bait hidden in the Satan's questions is the core issue of covenant faith, namely, the love that obtains between God and humanity. What covenant means is that God and human beings can be bound together in a relationship whose basic character is not instrumental—even though that relationship may be beneficial to human beings and pleasing to God.

Rather, covenant relationship is based on love that transcends self-interest on either side. At least, covenant is based on God's offering of such love and desire for a reciprocal response from us, and also on human aspiration to love God thus—even if that aspiration is unstable. But the Satan says there is no such thing as selfless love, and that means that the whole notion of covenant is nothing more than divine delusion. So when this naively told "folktale" is heard in the context of covenant theology, it is evident that what is at stake is the central claim of Israel's faith.

To test this claim, Job is methodically stripped of his herds and flocks, his servants, his sons and daughters. And sure enough, Job blesses the name of YHWH (1:21). Next, the sores that cover his body from head to foot make him a social outcast and seem to mark him as hated by God, yet Job says nothing at all. The silence is eerie, intolerable, and Job's wife rebels against it. She offers Job the words that will bring an end to his misery: "You still cling to your integrity? Curse God and die!" (2:9). Post-biblical Christian tradition has often made Mrs. Job out to be an unsympathetic shrew who imperils his soul. (The fourth-century Greek theologian St. John Chrysostom said that Job's greatest trial was that his wife was *not* taken.) But there is another way of hearing her words. Maybe she is not mocking his famous integrity at all, but rather appealing to it as the only fitting end to this divinely inflicted misery. "You still have a hold on your integrity. It's the one thing you have left, so put it to use. Your integrity demands that you curse the God who allowed our children to die." But Job refuses that way out. He answers curtly, "You're speaking as one of those who are spiritually unaware would speak. Shall we receive good at the hand of God and not receive evil?" The storyteller hints that there is now something ominous in Job's silence: "In all this, Job did not sin *with his lips*" (2:10)—a cautious statement, considering that earlier we were told he did not sin at all (1:22). The ancient rabbis inferred that with this, Job's first question, he had already begun to sin in his heart.[1] Now for the first time, Job has named God as the Source of evil.

It is well to note with care the silences in this book, for if its subject is good theology, what it means to "speak accurately about [God]" (42:8), then it must tell us something also about silence. It is odd to say that the most long-winded book in the Bible is about silence. Yet accurate speech about anything, and especially about God, is in fact a rhythm of silence and speech, speaking and listening. We come close to the central message of this book by following that rhythm, for by it Job's pain is gradually transformed into wholeness and peace.

The most important thing about Job's silence is that he does not remain alone in it. He is joined by three friends—Eliphaz, Bildad, and Zophar—who hear of Job's affliction and come from far off to comfort him.

> And they lifted up their eyes from a distance but could hardly recognize him. And they lifted up their voices and wept, and each one tore his robe and they threw dust over their heads into the air. And they sat with him on the ground seven days and seven nights without speaking a word to him, for they saw how great was his pain. (2:12-13)

Those seven days of silence are surely one of the most influential acts of pastoral care ever performed. The Jewish practice of "sitting *shiva*" (literally "sitting seven," when friends come to sit with mourners at home over the period of a week) memorializes the friends' wise compassion in this long moment of shared grief. More than twenty-five hundred years after the book of Job was written, this one act of Job's companions is imitated on a daily basis by comforters all over the world. Silence kept with others has a special quality. It is like a fine veil, preserving separateness, yet strangely heightening mutual awareness. Silence requires us to be present to the unexpressed needs of others, needs of which they may themselves not yet know. Cultivating the habit of silence should be seen as one of the special responsibilities of Christian community in a noisy world. It is a powerful means of fostering mutual encouragement among us, whom God has entrusted to one another in this wilderness of pain and doubt.

That week of shared silence is a period of transition for Job. In it he finds the words to speak his whole mind, to admit the pain of all that he has suffered. Considered in a pastoral context, "admitting pain" means two things. First, it means opening up a place for pain to do its work in our lives and then subside. Second, it means speaking honestly of pain, admitting it not just to ourselves but also to God, speaking our suffering as part of the confession of faith. Silence allows pain to penetrate our heart, "deep calling to deep" (Psalm 42:8). Silence comes to us in grief as the comforter of whom we are afraid, for it invites us more deeply into ourselves, into the dark places in which doubts emerge and pain becomes fully perceptible, where loss can no longer be denied. Silence is the friend who challenges us to be healed when we wish simply to be soothed. It heals us first by making us more empty, carving a space within our hearts, challenging us to—what? Trust that God will use that space and fill it with new life? No—Job's story forces us to put the matter more sharply. Trusting God is often a central preoccupation of the biblical writers, but not in this book. Rather, silence pushes Job to *challenge* God. When Job finds words at last, he demands steadily that God enter the abyss of loss and be revealed to him there.

Holding on Hard:
Job's Lament (Chapters 3-31)
The crowning blow to all Job's bitter losses is the intolerance of his friends. It is a tragic irony that they are unable to bear the words that their silent companionship helped him to find. Yet they should not be greatly blamed. Maybe in all literature, there are no more bitter words than those that fester and burst out of Job's silence:

> Why did I not die in the womb,
> emerge from the belly and expire?
> Why did knees receive me,
> and breasts give me suck?...
> Why does [God] give light to the wretched,
> and life to the bitter of soul;
> who wait for death—in vain;
> and dig for it rather than buried treasure;
> who would rejoice exceedingly,
> exult that they had found a grave?...
> For my sighs are my food;
> my groaning pours out like water....
> I have no rest, no quiet, no repose;
> turmoil has come. (3:11-12, 20-22, 24, 26)

There is something typically Israelite about the fact that Job's outburst begins with a repeated question, as he bitterly mimics the three-year-old's insistent "why": "Why didn't I die stillborn? Why does God give life to the bitter-hearted?" Job was a pious man before his tragedy, a godly man but not yet truly wise, for he did not know how much he did not understand. The radical not-knowing in his questions is the beginning of his wisdom.

Like any committed complainer, Job wants to lodge his accusations and demands directly with the responsible party. At the very beginning Job complains *about* God to his friends, but he very quickly gives up the third-party approach and lambasts God head-on. Here his questioning takes the form of a chilling parody of a well-known psalm (Psalm 8), one that praises the benevolent Creator for the unlikely mercy of caring about human beings. Finding no mercy, Job wishes God cared less:

> What is man that you make so much of him,
> and set your heart upon him;
> inspect him every morning,
> test him each moment? Will you never turn your
>   gaze from me,
> let me be till I swallow my spit? (7:17-19)

He goes on:

> Your hands fashioned and made me,
> and now you have turned and destroyed me.
> Remember, like clay you molded me;
> will you turn me back to dust? ...
> But this you hid in your heart
> (I know that this was your plan):
> If I should sin, you would be watching me,
> and not clear me of my offense! (10:8-9, 13-14)

From a theological standpoint, Job and his visitors have much common ground. They all hold the same belief system; they are committed to the idea that the universe operates according to a system of just deserts. The initial point of difference between Job and the others is that Job identifies a glitch in the system: he maintains that he is being punished in gross disproportion to any wrong he ever did. Although they begin with the same theological principle, Job and his would-be counselors develop it in very different ways. For Eliphaz, Bildad, and Zophar are academic theologians of the most speculative kind. They imagine that they can read God

130

like a book, and so they presume to tell Job precisely what God is doing, namely, disciplining or punishing him. But Job refuses absolutely to buy into their pat theories. Beginning in chapter 3 and almost to the very end of the book, Job will do his theological thinking at the top of his lungs, directing his shouts to God's face. His accusations are tactless, furious— yet in the end God will say that Job "has spoken accurately about me" (42:7-8), while his companions stand in need of Job's prayer precisely for their worthless prattling. In fact, the companions do say some things that sound like good theology. We even read excerpts from their speeches from time to time in church, and call it "the Word of the Lord." Yet the final divine judgment on them is that they are totally off base, because they are trying to talk *about* God without engaging in the fearsome, always potentially disorienting business of talking directly *to* God. Therefore their words can only "bloom like cut flowers."[2] When God speaks out of the whirlwind, they all blow away.

The protracted arguments of Job's interlocutors may well bore us, and probably they should. It is like watching Samuel Beckett's *Waiting for Godot:* nothing changes and no one moves forward. By the end of the play, if you are not faint with the excruciating tedium of it all, then you missed the point. For anyone who hopes to bring comfort to a person in pain, the lesson to be derived from this long central section of Job is mostly negative: our role as comforters is not to solve the problem of pain; even less is it to stick up for God. Trying to vindicate God to a person in agonizing pain is like explaining to a crying infant that Mommy is really a well-intentioned person. The friends' words do not help Job. Nonetheless, something does begin to happen as they rehearse their arguments. While the others remain mired in their convictions, Job is moving. Though immersed in pain, he is not stuck. What goads and guides him through his pain is simply the determination not to let God off the hook for a moment. Eventually Job's determination to hold God accountable to himself becomes his hope of redemption:

> I know that my Redeemer lives,...
> and from my flesh [without my flesh?]³ I shall gaze
>   on God,
> upon whom I shall gaze for myself—
> and my eyes see, and not a stranger. (19:25-27)

131

What, after all, generates Job's hope of seeing God, when nothing has changed for him, when no one has brought him any real comfort? This book of Job hints at a strange truth that is never explained, and probably cannot be explained: the full admission of pain opens the door to hope. The Peruvian poet Cesar Vallejo writes about a pain so simple, so consuming, that it has "neither a father nor a son"—no cause, no explanation. It illumines nothing and produces no insight. The prose-poem is an unbroken lament. It ends with the words: "Today I am in pain, no matter what happens. Today I am simply in pain." Yet Vallejo gives his poem a title that points beyond the lament. It is called "I am going to talk about hope."⁴ Maybe the very act of finding words for pain—and especially beautiful words, like those of Vallejo and the Joban poet—breeds hope, hope that someone (Someone?) is listening and might care.

Initially, Job says that it is hopeless to argue with God:

> If one wanted to contend with him,
> one could not answer him one time out of a
>   thousand....
> Even if I am innocent, my own mouth would
>   condemn me;
> I am a person of integrity, but he would make me
>   perverse. (9:3, 20)

Yet Job keeps talking, and gradually he grows in confidence that he can make his case:

> Look, I have set my case in order;
> I know that I am in the right....
> Call, and I myself shall answer;
> or I shall speak, and you respond to me. (13:18, 22)

The next step is his growing hope that there is indeed Someone to corroborate his case:

> Even now, look, in the heavens is my witness,
> and the one who testifies for me is in the heights.
> (16:19)

Slowly and fitfully, Job's hope of making his case before God grows. Often he lapses back into despair. But his movement in and through pain may be measured also by the expansion of his vision beyond his own personal situation. Although he begins in fetal position, wishing himself back into nonexistence, he opens his eyes to see that his agony is not unique. The suffering of the innocent is in fact rampant—something he did not notice so much when he himself was fortunate. So Job gradually moves from fetal position to prophetic stance, denouncing the ease and prosperity of the wicked (21:7-34). Now his own suit is part of a larger case for the cause of the just (24:1-25), for whom he is the bold spokesman:

> Even today my speech is defiance;
> [God's] hand is heavy despite my groaning.
> If only I knew where to find him,
> I would come to his tribunal.
> I would lay my case before him and fill my mouth
>   with arguments....
> Would he use great force to contend with me?
> No, surely he would heed me.

> There the upright could reason with him,
> and I would finally be acquitted in my suit.
>
> (23:2-4, 6-7)

The divine Judge from whom Job expects acquittal is, of course, the same God whom he accuses of injustice. With a passion for justice instilled by God, he turns the prophetic demand for vindication of the righteous *against* God. Here is the acute paradox that lies at the heart of this book, and also the reason the church is afraid of it: Job rails against God, not as a skeptic, not as a stranger to God's justice, but precisely as a believer.[5] It is the very depth of Job's commitment to God's ethical vision that makes his rage so fierce, and that will finally compel an answer from God.

Goethe expresses a desperate but strong way of laying hold of God that is unknown to most contemporary Christians:

> And so at last the sailor lays firm hold
> upon the rock on which he had been dashed.[6]

We are not accustomed to blaming God, and so when we find ourselves doing so, we feel guilty and religiously confused. The "solution," for some, is to cover our confusion about God with a false piety. Others, bolder perhaps, will give up on God altogether. But the witness of the book of Job is that rage and even blame directed at God are valid moments in the life of faith. Further, the very fact that Job's outcry extends over so many chapters tells us that we may stay in that "moment" for a long time.

Some few believers in every generation have always lived in the acute paradox of holding on to God, and at the same time blaming God for their suffering. In the present age, probably those who have struggled most courageously and faithfully with this are Jews, whom the deadly storm of the Holocaust[7] has cast upon God the Rock (Psalm 19:15).

Yosl Rakover Talks to God is one modern expression of that dangerous rage of the faithful. It is the last testament of a fictional Jew dying in the Warsaw Ghetto uprising.

134

> I die at peace, but not pacified, conquered and beaten but not enslaved, bitter but not disappointed, a believer but not a suppliant, a lover of God but not His blind Amen-sayer.

> I have followed Him, even when he pushed me away. I have obeyed His commandments, even when He scourged me for it. I have loved him, I have been in love with Him and remained so, even when He made me lower than the dust, tormented me to death, abandoned me to shame and mockery....

> Here, then, are my last words to You, my angry God: None of this will avail you in the least! You have done everything to make me lose my faith in you, to make me cease to believe in You. But I die exactly as I have lived, an unshakeable [sic] believer in You.[8]

Job ends his lament by relapsing into a deep silence immediately after he concludes his lengthy final defense speech (chapters 29–31). Having demolished the contention of Eliphaz, Bildad, and Zophar that Job is grossly, albeit secretly, wicked, he will not be provoked to further words by any "quack doctors" of theology (13:4). The newcomer Elihu shows up and, disgusted with the failure of the others to refute Job, he offers a half-dozen chapters of his own theology of suffering, some of it quite good. But still Job says nothing. He will not speak again until theology has been renewed from the Source.

God's Speech and Job's Transformation
(Chapters 38-42)
God begins the renewal of speech about God's ways exactly
as Job began his complaint, with a series of questions:

> Who is this who darkens design
> by words without knowledge?
> Gird your loins like a hero;
> I will ask you; now you tell me! Where were you
> when I founded the earth?
> Tell me if you have understanding:
> who fixed its dimensions—surely you know!
> Or who stretched out over it a measuring line?
>
> (38:2-5)

Many readers see God's answer from the whirlwind as
pure bluster and no answer at all. God just rolls out that big
Creation Machine and mows Job down with a stream of *non
sequiturs* that have nothing to do with what is really at stake.
If Job finally stops talking altogether, then it is not because
he is persuaded by anything God has said, but simply
because there is no point in arguing with a bully.

It is true that God does not give a direct answer to Job's
urgent suit about the prosperity of the wicked and the suffering of the innocent, nor even bother to refute Job's
implied charge of mismanagement in the moral sphere. On
the contrary, God agrees that the persistence of the wicked is
a knotty problem—and if Job can figure out how to get rid
of them, then bully for him:

> Then even I will praise you,
> that your right hand has won you victory!
> Look now, here's Behemoth, whom I made along
> with you. (40:14-15)

God simply passes over the moral issue as Job has posed it and directs his attention elsewhere, to something that seems to interest God more just now, namely, the non-human elements of the universe. The two great poems that constitute God's speech offer Job a completely different view of reality, a God's-eye view of the world that takes no direct account of his own personal situation. Yet in the end, Job acknowledges that he has seen God and, further, that he is satisfied with God's response to his suit. Job's one unyielding claim, held to the bitter end of his lament (27:5), is that he is indeed "a man of integrity" (1:1), as God said at the very beginning. The divine speeches do at the end uphold that claim—but they do so obliquely, in the manner typical of poetry. Yet at the same time, they completely transform Job's own understanding of what his integrity must entail.

The Rabbis have a saying: "The question of a wise person is half an answer." How much more so, when the One asking questions is the only One, as the book of Job tells us, who really knows where wisdom is to be found (28:20-28)?

> Who cut for the torrent a channel,
> and a path for the thunderbolts;
> to make it rain on earth with not a person in it,
> desert with no one there,
> to satisfy the wild waste
> and bring forth a crop of grass? (38:25-27)

"To make it rain on earth with not a person in it"—that one phrase says a lot about the way God runs things. And what it says is a calculated offense to ordinary human expectations. Remember that in ancient Israel, life depended directly on the precarious, never-too-abundant rainfall. No one wastes water in the arid climate of the Middle East—no one except God. God relishes extravagant gestures, as does Cyrano de Bergerac, but goes him one better. Cyrano flings a purse of gold coins at the crowd; God flings rain on the desert, where no one even cheers. They do it for kicks.

Just about as sensible as watering the wasteland is God's delight in the wild creatures. He proudly displays the mountain goats that give birth in impenetrable recesses, the desert ass that roams far from the herdsman's shout, the wild ox that scorns to plow a field, the silly happy ostrich. All these creatures in the divine photo album have one thing in common: they are completely untamable. Every animal in which God glories is utterly useless, except the war horse, and that is the exception that proves the rule. You may use him, God says of the snorting horse impatient for battle, but don't imagine you can master him!

This God's-eye view of the world plays havoc with Job's notion of the way things ought to be—which is to say, sensible, well-adapted to human purposes, and above all, predictable. From the beginning we see that Job is extraordinarily punctilious in his religious observances. He is "God-fearing" in the extreme. Remember those preemptive sacrifices that Job used to offer each year on behalf of his children, *just in case* they had sinned (1:5)? Again, his final defense speech shows Job to be a self-consciously exemplary husband and father, a man who is kind to the poor, true to God, and responsible in looking out for his servants—which, we might infer, is more than God can say.

Job is convinced that his moral innocence should have warded off disaster, because he believes that the world is a manageable place run by a demanding but nonetheless predictable God who owes the righteous a good time. But when God finally speaks and shows Job what, from a divine perspective, is so fascinating about the created order, it turns out to have nothing at all to do with human moral standards. Here, for instance, is the ostrich, who forgets where her own eggs are buried and steps right on them—but when she flies, there's a sight! She is the comic book anti-type to Job's own anxious style of parenting.

God's involvement with the world expresses itself in huge, unapologetic delight in a creation whose outstanding quality is quite simply magnificence: power and freedom on a scale that is bewildering and terrifying. The great symbols of that magnificence are, of course, Leviathan and Behemoth. From a human perspective, they are monstrous aberrations: an overblown crocodile and a customized hippo. Modern commentators often compare them to ancient Near Eastern chaos monsters, the troublemakers in the universe, who must be destroyed in order to make the world habitable for decent creatures like us. But that is hardly how God sees these big guys. They are, it seems, the top of the creation line, and God speaks of them with intense pride. Behemoth, God tells Job, is "the best thing I ever did" (40:19); and every one of Leviathan's scales was set in place with the same exquisite care (41:15-17) that fashioned Job in the womb.

Now why should God love a world like that? Annie Dillard provides an excellent answer: because "the creator loves pizzazz." She is reflecting not on Leviathan and Behemoth, but on all their strange kin who share the world with us:

> The world is full of creatures that for some reasons seem stranger to us than others, and libraries are full of books describing them—hagfish, platypuses, lizardlike pangolins four feet long with bright green, lapped scales like umbrella-tree leaves on a bush hut root, butterflies emerging from anthills, spiderlings wafting through the air clutching tiny silken balloons, horseshoe crabs...the creator creates. Does he stoop, does he speak, does he save, succor, prevail? Maybe. But he creates; he creates everything and anything.

The creator goes off on one wild, specific tangent after another, or millions simultaneously, with an exuberance that would seem to be unwarranted, and with an abandoned energy sprung from an unfathomable font. What is going on here? The point of the dragonfly's terrible lip, the giant water bug, birdsong, or the beautiful dazzle and flash of sunlighted minnows, is not that it all fits together like clockwork—for it doesn't, not even inside the goldfish bowl—but that it all flows so freely wild, like the creek, that it all surges in such a free, fringed tangle. Freedom is the world's water and weather, the world's nourishment freely given, its soil and sap: and the creator loves pizzazz.[9]

I quote at length because this is a point we are slow to get. We are so accustomed to thinking of God in sober terms. We are comfortable talking about God's sound *moral* character— "merciful and gracious, slow to anger, and abounding in steadfast love and faithfulness" (Exodus 34:6). But the idea that God might have *aesthetic* preferences is strange; it seems frivolous, beneath God's dignity. Yet the speech out of the whirlwind would seem to suggest that God does indeed exhibit a certain style, and admire it in the creatures. Moreover, God's moral and aesthetic preferences belong together. Love of pizzazz is compatible with an aspect of God's moral character with which we are familiar: God's self-giving generosity. What God shows Job is the highest form of causality operative in the universe, the generosity that brings another into free being. Yet it costs something truly to delight in the freedom of the beloved, as any parent knows. The Bible as a whole gives us a fairly good idea of what it costs God to create and preserve a world of creatures who are beautiful—and dangerous—precisely in their unpredictability.

And what does all this mean for Job's case? Job has long clung to his "integrity" (27:5), by which he meant being responsible within his own social sphere. But now that God has given this guided tour of the creation, the whole project of human integrity looks different. It means fitting into a design vastly bigger and more complex than Job ever imagined. What God says, in effect, is this: "Look away from yourself, Job; look around you. For a moment see the world with my eyes, in all its intricacy and wild beauty. The beauty is in the wildness, Job; you cannot tame all that frightens you without losing the beauty." God calls this man of integrity to take his place in a ravishing but dangerous world where only those who relinquish their personal expectations can live in peace. The price of peace is the surrender of our personal expectations, which are always too small for the huge freedom built into the system.

The great question that God's speech out of the whirlwind poses for Job and every other person of integrity is this: Can you love what you do not control? That implied question is only another form of the one that the Satan put to God at the very beginning: "Is it for no good reason that Job serves God?" The shocking revelation out of the whirlwind is that God gets a kick out of doing things for no good reason at all—making it rain on the desert, for instance, with no one there. The truth that Job never suspected is that gratuitousness is one of the hidden values of creation.

Job's answer to that revelation is a deepening of silence. Citing God's earlier questions (see 38:2-3, page 135), he now acknowledges the insufficiency of all his words:

"Who is this who obscures design without
    knowledge?"
Yes, I talked but did not understand,
of things too wondrous for me, that I did not know.
"Listen now and I will speak; I will ask and you

tell me!"[10]
I had heard of you by hearsay,
but now my eye has seen you.
Therefore I recant and change my mind
concerning dust and ashes. (42:3-6)

These last two lines are crucial for understanding what has happened to Job. The verse is generally translated along these lines:

therefore I despise myself,
and repent in dust and ashes. (NRSV)

Yet the Hebrew verb translated "repent" denotes any kind of mental and emotional reorientation, either positive or negative; "repentance" is only one possibility. Moreover, the phrase "dust and ashes" always appears in the Bible as a metaphor, not as a reference to literal dust heaps. The metaphor consistently designates the humbleness of the human condition, seen in light of God's majesty (see Genesis 18:27). Therefore, it is highly unlikely that Job is abasing himself before God here, as the traditional translation suggests. If Job now has little to say, then this is the silence not of self-disgust, but of desire fulfilled. Job has gotten what he most wanted: he has seen God. And as a result he takes a new view of the human condition and of his own place in the world. Job's silence at the end of the book bespeaks his spiritual transformation. It is not only his theology that is renewed; it is his whole mind.

In fact, the clearest expression of the renewal of Job's mind is not anything he says. It is his willingness to have more children. I have heard it said in modern Israel that the most courageous act of faith the Jews have ever performed was to have babies after the Holocaust, to trust God with more defenseless children. The note at the end of the book

142

that Job had seven sons and three daughters is often considered to be a cheap parting shot—as though God could make it all up by giving Job another set of children to replace the ones who were lost. But that is to judge the last scene of the book from the wrong side. This book is not about justifying God's actions; it is about Job's transformation. It is useless to ask how much (or how little) it costs God to give more children. The real question is how much it costs Job to become a father again. How can he open himself again to the terrible vulnerability of loving those whom he cannot protect against suffering and untimely death?

Of course, we never get a direct answer to that question. But here is a hint that tells us something about what kind of father Job becomes, after all his grief. It is in the strange detail about him naming his daughters: "He called the name of the one *Yemima* (Dove) and the name of the second *Ketsia* (Cinnamon) and the name of the third *Keren-haPuch* (Horn of Eye-Shadow)" (42:14). Sensuous names are not the biblical norm, and naming a daughter for a cosmetic is way over the top. But there is more: "And there were not to be found throughout the whole land women as beautiful as Job's daughters, and their father gave them an inheritance alongside their brothers" (42:15). In the male-dominated societies of the ancient world, it is an affront for a father blessed with many sons to leave anything to daughters. So once-cautious Job is now overturning all the rules, and as for a reason— well, the only thing we know is that Dove, Cinnamon, and Horn of Eye-Shadow were exceptionally pretty women. Which is to say, Job does it for no good reason at all. He does it just for kicks.

The two portraits of Father Job that stand at either end of this book mark the true measure of his transformation. Job, this man of integrity who was once so careful, fearful of God and of the *possible* sins of his children, becomes at the last freewheeling, breaking with custom to honor daughters alongside sons, bestowing inheritances and snappy names. The inspiration and model for this wild style of parenting is, of course, God the Creator. Job learned about it when God spoke out of the whirlwind. And now Job loves with the abandon characteristic of God's love—revolutionary in seeking our freedom, reveling in the untamed beauty of every child.

143

Notes

1. Talmud, Baba Batra 16a.

2. The phrase comes from Karl Barth's luminous interpretation of Job: *Church Dogmatics,* vol. IV/3.1 (Edinburgh: T & T Clark, 1961), 457.

3. The Hebrew poetry of this line (like many others in the book of Job) is ambiguous and open to several interpretations. It is not clear whether Job expects to see God before or after his own death.

4. Robert Bly, ed., *Neruda and Vallejo: Selected Poems* (Boston: Beacon Press, 1971), 243.

5. This is the insight of Karl Barth, *Church Dogmatics,* IV/3.1, 404.

6. Goethe, *Tasso,* quoted by Karl Barth, ibid., 424.

7. The modern Hebrew term used to designate the Nazi Holocaust is *sho'ah.* In the Bible, the word denotes a great storm.

8. Zvi Kolitz, *Yosl Rakover Talks to God,* trans. Carol Brown Janeway (New York: Pantheon Books, 1999), 23-24.

9. Annie Dillard, *Pilgrim at Tinker Creek* (New York: Harper & Row, 1974), 136-137.

10. This could also be a citation of Job's own bold call to God in 13:22.

PART FOUR

HABITS OF THE HEART

THE THEOLOGY OF the Bible is concrete rather than speculative. On every page the biblical writers take up the wholly practical question of what we need to do every day in order to live intimately and well with God. The fourth part of this book shows how Old Testament texts treat the daily disciplines of our life with God. These are not what we normally think of as religious disciplines—for example, fasting once a week, or through Lent—useful though those may be. Rather, once we start reading in a spiritually engaged way, it is evident that the Old Testament is urging us toward certain habits of heart and mind that "work" in our relationship with God. It encourages us to cultivate countercultural habits such as seeking solitude, or repenting of our sins, or offering praise to God; new dispositions such as looking for the sheer pleasure of God's company, or turning to God to listen as much as to speak. I will not say that these habits make it *easier* to be involved with God (the biblical writers never make that claim), but they deepen our involvement and make it more profitable to our souls.

CHAPTER ELEVEN

DESIRABLE DISCIPLINE

Proverbs 8

THE SAGES OF ANCIENT Israel imagined wisdom as a woman whose public behavior was, by the standards of their society, aggressive in the extreme. In Proverbs 8 she takes her stand by the city gate, the place where the street vendors hawk their goods; where street preachers set up soap boxes; where a teacher hangs up a shingle, hoping to recruit a few students to his struggling house of study. At times Wisdom herself sounds like a vendor or a soap-box preacher, but mostly she sounds like a teacher—that is, a teacher of the old school, who addresses her potential students bluntly:

> I'm calling you folks;
> my voice is for human beings.
> You ignorant ones, get some insight into intelligent
> behavior.
> Fools, get heart and mind ready! (8:4-5)

In fact she sounds very much like my high school Latin teacher—likewise a teacher of the old school, who did not suffer fools gladly. Yet I would not say that Mr. Kuehnl lacked concern for us, even compassion. We know compassion by its fruits, and he shaped my life profoundly. From him I learned to submit my mind to discipline. He taught me that not chiefly because he was strict (though God knows he was), but because he cultivated in me a desire. I *wanted* the language he taught. Through Latin I saw the opportunity to enter into what seemed to me a vastly expanded world, a world with more dimensions than I could discover in my small-town, high-school environs.

The point is that Mr. Kuehnl could help me acquire intellectual discipline because he taught me to desire something I had not wanted before. That is, I think, what every great teacher does, including and above all Lady Wisdom herself. It is noteworthy that the Israelite sages portrayed wisdom as a woman, and at times this Lady Wisdom is a distinctly alluring figure, although she is never a soft touch. Nonetheless, she is a figure designed to awaken desire in young males, namely, the students of the Israelite sages. But if we heed her, then she can also help us sober post-adolescents desire something we do not now desire, or do not desire enough: the discipline of wisdom. Listen to her:

> Take my discipline, and not silver;
> knowledge is more choice than fine gold. (8:10)

Wisdom's discipline is rare and valuable, but difficult, more difficult even than learning Latin paradigms. So in order to awaken in us keen desire for her discipline, Lady Wisdom speaks to us in the language of love and longing:

> Those who love me, I love,...
> granting my lovers an inheritance of real substance.
> (8:17, 21)

The sages represent "her" as the ultimate in desirability:

> For Wisdom is better than rubies,
> and no other desire can compare with her. (8:11)

The erotic language that evokes Lady Wisdom may be an effective ploy to get adolescents to study, but it is more than that. It is a source of genuine religious insight. In using the language of love and desire, the sages alert us to the hidden but essential connection between what we want and what we may come to know. Those two things are always connected, for good or for ill. Through holy desire we may indeed gain what Israel called wisdom, which is a true, realistic knowledge of God, ourselves, and the world. But we may also waste our desire, by turning it to things that are unworthy of us. Or perhaps we desire things that are good in themselves, but they are not the things that God wants to give us now. So our desire, which is meant to draw us closer to God, instead sets a barrier between God and ourselves. For desire is never spiritually neutral. It either sharpens our perception, so that we may see something of what God sees in us and the world, or else it distorts our vision. In countless subtle ways, wrong desire skews our understanding of our God-given situation in the world. In other words, wrong desire deprives us of wisdom and thus brings us, often by slow degrees, into misery.

This connnection between desire and wisdom is so fundamental to our nature that it is highlighted at the beginning of the Bible, in the third chapter of Genesis. That connection lies at the heart of what we call "the Fall," which (contrary to what we might think) has everything to do with desire and nothing to do with sex. The Garden of Eden was the place where the first human creatures might have acquired wisdom: Eden was the place for total intimacy with God, and that is the sole condition for becoming wise. Day by day they might have grown in wisdom and stature, taking those strolls with God in "the breezy time of day" (Genesis 3:8). But they could not wait to get smart, so they chose the quick and dirty method recommended by the snake. And the biblical narra-

149

tor shows us that moment of choice through Eve's eyes. It is very rare for the Bible to tell us what someone is thinking; usually we hear only what they say or do. But now we stand with Eve and see exactly as she saw in that fateful moment:

> And the woman *saw* that the tree was good for eating and that it was *desirable to the eyes;* and the tree was to be *coveted* for making smart. And she took from its fruit, and she ate. (Genesis 3:6)

"Thou shall not covet." Unholy desire leads to distorted perception of self, world, and God. Eve and Adam ate, and their eyes were indeed opened (Genesis 3:7), but they no longer saw the goodness of the situation in which God had placed them. What they saw instead was their nakedness, the poverty of their situation. Now they saw God as someone to hide from. Each of them looked around for someone to blame.

The story of Adam and Eve is not a story of something that happened once, long, long ago. Like every true myth, it is a story of what happens to women and men even now, over and over again. Wrong desire separates us from God. It blinds us to the goodness of the situations in which God has placed us. It separates us from one another. We may indeed learn something from following wrong desire, but too often what we come to know about the world and about ourselves embitters us. From this downward spiral of wrong desire and bitter knowledge, Lady Wisdom seeks to free us. Like every great and demanding teacher, she asks us to discipline our eyes so that we may look at the world in a new way and conceive a new set of desires. Holy Wisdom asks us to engage in a vigorous act of reimagination, so that we may see clearly that knowledge of God *is* lovelier than gold, that wisdom is better than rubies or any other delight on which we could possibly fix our wandering gaze.

When will we ever be wise? For us the true measure of our wisdom will never be the grade point average we covet, a degree or rank, the right job, the book accepted by a prestigious press. No, we will be wise when we desire with heart, soul, mind, and strength only the things that God also desires for us—and nothing else compels us, or even catches our wandering eye. Try to imagine it:

> • *I will be wise when my greed is gone.* When I have abandoned my present practice of consuming far more than I need of the good things of this world, when my eyes do not linger on the object that was produced in a sweatshop in a country whose environment is degraded and economy desperate—then I will be wise.

> • *I will be wise when my compassion is pure.* When a piece of gossip dies of neglect in my mind and no word of searing criticism springs to my lips; when I earnestly desire the healing of my persecutor, not her humiliation; when I feel pure joy at the blessing another enjoys—then I will be wise.

> • *I will be wise when my love is constant,* so that I never look slightingly on those who depend upon my love, nor look at anyone with wrong desire.

> • *I will be wise when I hunger and thirst for righteousness,* when I truly see my talents, energies, and resources as God sees them: as means not to secure my own position, but to strengthen the weak, comfort the downcast, empower those whose lives mine touches.

When what I desire in all and above all else is
the company of God,
the coming of Christ,
the comfort of the Holy Spirit,
then I will be wise.

We have a long way to go, most of us, and worship can help us along the way. For it is in the act of worship that the church steadily renews itself in the discipline of wisdom. Worship is a vigorous act of reordering our desires in the light of God's burning desire for the wellness of all creation. In song and prayer we articulate holy desires, although we may not yet feel them in our bones. We repent of unholy desires that are still eating away at us, and through us, eating at others. We are not yet wise, but we take part in worship so that through scripture we may study what *God* desires for this groaning yet grace-filled world, and in prayer we may grow and change, until *we* burn with like desire.

CHAPTER TWELVE

A FOOL FOR LOVE

Exodus 33

And Moses said to the LORD, "Look, you say to me, 'Bring this people up,' yet you have not let me know whom you will send with me. And you, you said, 'I know you by name, and indeed you have found favor in my eyes.' And now, if I have really found favor in your eyes, then let me know your way, so that *I* may know *you*, in order that I may find favor in your eyes. And look—this nation is really *your* people!" (Exodus 33:12-13)

AS FAR AS I KNOW, this passage from Exodus is the earliest recorded account we have of pastoral burnout. It tells of a time when Moses lost all energy and interest in bringing the Israelites out of bondage in Egypt and into God's service—that perfect freedom which demands so much more emotional and spiritual maturity than does slavery. We see him now, only a few months into the forty-year journey in the wilderness, and already he is worn out by this "mongrel lot" of former slaves. Moses has a right to be exhausted, disgusted with these hopeless ingrates. These last four months in the desert they have been awash in the wonders of God's immediate presence: accompanying them as a pillar of cloud by day and fire by night, leading them across the dry floor of the Red Sea, feeding them with manna in the moonscape wilderness of Sinai, bringing forth water from flintrock to assuage their thirst. Only six weeks ago God spoke to them the words of life from Sinai. Moses wrote those words and sealed the covenant with the blood of sacrifice, blood splashed on the altar and on the Israelites, marking them as God's own forever.

For their sakes, Moses spent forty days and forty nights on Sinai, fasting and listening, purifying the channels of his ears and his heart so that he might be a clear conduit for God's Teaching. But the restless Israelites found those six weeks of waiting upon God's word too long, so they melted down their gold earrings into a little holy cow while Moses' brother Aaron presided as high priest over the whole debacle. Thus the people made themselves detestable, and now God tells Moses to get them out of his face:

> Go on, go up from here, you and this people which you brought up from the land of Egypt.... to a land flowing with milk and honey. For I must not go up in your midst, since you are a stiff-necked people, lest I eat you up on the road. If I went up in your midst even for one second, I would wipe you out. (33:1,3)

No wonder Moses plunges to the bottom. He is disgusted with the Israelites, betrayed by his own brother, and now even God has bailed out, leaving him alone with a job he never wanted to take on in the first place. It certainly was not his idea to bring this people out of Egypt. For, as Moses reminds God when they have it out in a frank talk at the Tent of Meeting, "Look, this nation is your people after all!" I think it must be for his frankness that Moses is so beloved of

God. This conversation at the Tent of Meeting is the most intimate exchange between the two of them that we are privileged to witness. Actually, it is more like a domestic quarrel. Moses and God are like a long-married couple whose children are in a particularly trying phase of their development, and the kids' problems are taking a big toll on their relationship. So here the great shepherd of Israel launches his gripe against the Deity:

> "Look," you say to me, "Bring this people up"—and you haven't even told me whom you're going to send with me! And yet you yourself said, "I know you by name, and you have found favor in my eyes." And now, if I've really found favor in your eyes, then show me your way, that I may know you, so that I may find favor in your eyes. (33:12-13)

Four times Moses expresses his anxiety to find favor in God's eyes; three times he cajoles God to escort them personally to Canaan. Forget the angel: it won't do. And even after God caves in and says, "All right, all right, I'll come"— still Moses keeps at it: "And if you don't come, then you can just leave us here." Some think this *non sequitur* and all the repetitions betray the hand of a hack editor who briefly had a job writing for the Bible, but they miss the point: Moses is panic-stricken, too frantic to take in what God is saying. So he keeps trampling over the same muddy piece of ground, harping on the same demand.

This state of mind, I suspect, is not unfamiliar to any of us in our private life with God. As Christians, we are all engaged in the business of discerning and obeying God's call, and this usually means that soon enough we find ourselves out beyond our own competence, frightened at what God demands and feeling cosmically abandoned, left in the lurch with a job for which our own resources are completely

155

inadequate. Every persistent believer must reckon with that sense of fear and divine abandonment. Sooner or later, the panic touches each one of us who accepts God's call and heads, eyes wide open, straight into some difficult and mysterious work—like pastoring a church, teaching a class, going back to school, learning a language, creating a work of art. The panic descends on everyone who accepts God's call to do something that engages our heart and wracks our soul—like making a marriage prosper through better and worse, raising a child and letting her go into adulthood, enduring a terrible illness, growing up, growing old.

Being called out far beyond our own competence is in fact part of our regular experience with God; therefore we have a particular interest in how Moses' panic attack is calmed. The breakthrough comes when he makes that outrageous request: "Show me your glory" (33:18). I am sure Moses surprised himself with that rash, even crude demand. For it is crude, completely lacking in religious refinement. Moses wants God to strut his stuff for him—a private showing of the divine being. Even more shocking than the request is the fact that God goes along with it, so what follows is a scene like something out of Greek mythology: Moses hides in the rock while God strolls past in something very much like a body, singing a hymn, and Moses gets a look at the divine backside. Yet even that hindsight of blinding beauty makes him fall on his face in awe.

It is a weird scene, to say the least. We have to ask, why does God condescend to this—the God of Israel, who is notoriously averse to being pinned down to any bodily form? A burning bush, a pillar of cloud or fire, a thunderous voice from a mountaintop—these are as close as God normally gets to physical manifestation. So why does our customarily elusive God now consent to this undignified parade, with a physicality that borders on immodesty? I can only guess at an answer. Graven images are a lie, because they delude us into thinking that we have a line on God and know just what to expect. Fixed images of God violate what is most characteristic of God: free-spiritedness. That was the very first truth God revealed to Moses out of the burning bush, with the Name that bespeaks God's radical freedom: *'ehyeh 'asher 'ehyeh,* "I will be who I will be" (Exodus 3:14).

God hates being taken for granted, and in that we have a clue to this strange concession. For above all else God is a Lover, and every true lover resists being taken for granted yet longs to be desired. "Show me your glory." God goes along with the request because, frankly, God is flattered. At this moment, it is not Moses the religious-political leader of Israel speaking, but Moses the mystic, the ardent lover of God. The public need has been met: God has promised twice already to go up with the people into the Promised Land. You would think Moses would be satisfied, but instead he presses for one more thing: a favor for himself alone, a glimpse of God's exquisite beauty. Of course God is flattered. Who would not be thrilled to know that a lover through many years and many domestic crises still finds one desirable, desirable just for oneself, when the children's needs have been met and there is nothing to be sought or gained but the simple joy of intimacy? It is only in that request for a private revelation that God feels the purity of Moses' love. Of course God capitulates, happily, even to the point of indignity. For as the whole Bible makes undeniably clear, God is a perfect fool for love—fool enough even to become human, to live and love as we do, and to weep because he loves; fool enough to suffer and die on a cross.

All our weariness in being "good Christians" comes from forgetting this, the perfect foolishness of God in love, and therefore our prayers become disordered. Like Moses, the very best of us grow impatient, sometimes desperate, trying to do the manifold work God has given us, and seeing that the results are often indifferent. We demand support for our efforts, reasoning, as Moses does, that it is in God's enlightened self-interest to back us up in our work—so that the church may look good, so that God may look good, so that the people of God may be well served. There is evidence that God responds to those prayers and often does support our good works. Yet the encounter at the Tent of Meeting suggests that God is even more deeply moved by holy desire: "Show me your glory." God is strangely stirred by the unreasonable demand of the one who burns with love, who longs simply to revel in the incomparable divine beauty that all the saints have glimpsed and that left them panting with desire for more.

God's beauty is not a pleasure reserved for great saints and card-carrying mystics, religious geniuses who speak in blank verse. The most tongue-tied, feet-on-the-ground believer is capable of getting a kick out of God—and needs to do so. The reason is simple: it is the very pleasure for which we are made. In a well-known statement of Christian anthropology, the Westminster Confession of Faith gives the purpose of human life thus: "to glorify God and to enjoy him forever." Enjoying God is a trait of the species, like being a biped, no more technically complex than enjoying sunshine or wisteria. As with wisteria and sunshine, though, we must slow down enough to notice, so that the quiet but nonetheless thrilling "pleasantness of God" may sink into our chilled hearts, refresh our jaded eyes with a warmth and beauty that knows no season. The psalmist has given us a prayer that establishes the proper order for what we ask of God, if we are to remain strong in God's service:

> May the pleasantness of the LORD our God be
> upon us;

and the work of our hands, make it prosper for us;
the work of our hands, O prosper it. (Psalm 90:17)

First pleasure, then work. Pleasure for ourselves in God's
company, God's beauty, and only then support for our work   159
in God's service.

CHAPTER THIRTEEN

"LIKE GRASS I'M DRIED UP"

Psalm 102

My days are gone up in smoke
and my bones burn like a furnace.
My heart is stricken, like grass, dried up,
I am too wasted to eat my bread.
Because of my loud groaning,
my bone sticks to my skin. (Psalm 102:4-5)

THAT CRIES OF PAIN like this are to be found in the
Bible is one of the best-kept secrets of the Christian faith. We
do not hear them much on Sunday mornings. Many regular
churchgoers have no idea that laments like these exist, and so
when the lives of Christians plummet to the bottom, they are
deprived of any useful prayer.

A young priest visited one of her parishioners in the
nursing home where he was living. He would neither speak
to her nor look at her; he simply glared straight ahead. Her
pastoral instincts were good, so she did not try to engage him
in chitchat, but went straight for the psalms. She read him

psalms of comfort: "The LORD is my shepherd." "My help comes from the LORD, the maker of heaven and earth." "Like a child upon its mother's breast, my soul is quieted within me." But the words of comfort elicited no response—just the same stony stare. So as a last resort, she began reading from the laments:

I have become like a vulture in the wilderness,
like an owl among the ruins. . . .
I eat ashes like bread and mix my drink with tears,
because of your indignation and anger,
because you [God] have picked me up and tossed
    me aside. (Psalm 102:7, 10-11)

At those words the stony face softened. For the first time, the man looked at his visitor and said, "Finally, somebody who knows how I feel!"

Somebody who knows how I feel—and isn't too polite to say it, to say it in God's face. That is the value of the lament psalms. Like the man in the nursing home, the poet who wrote Psalm 102 knows just how it feels to have lost everything that made life dear, everything that made him recognizable to himself. For Jerusalem is destroyed—Jerusalem, more precious than every other joy in life. Jerusalem so dear that, as the psalmist cries in anguish, "Your servants hold even her rubble precious and her dust they cherish!" (102:15). Jerusalem is rubble, and the psalmist's own life is as good as finished:

My days are like a declining shadow;
and I—like grass I'm dried up.
But you, O LORD, forever you sit enthroned,
and your remembrance is from generation to
    generation. (102:12-13)

162

My withered life versus God's eternity—the psalmist is obsessed with that stark and terrible contrast. God enthroned forever, and the holy city Jerusalem in rubble. These two are radically incompatible; they literally cannot be held together in Israelite thought. Yet everything depends upon bringing them together. This is no theoretical problem, but the most pressing existential one—and not just for some ancient Israelite poet, but also for us. We worship an eternal God. And what does that mean to us who are living, all of us, in the midst of death? To put it in the terms the psalmists use: Can God who is "from everlasting to everlasting" (Psalm 103:17) really be *my* God? Can God the Rock (the psalmists' most common metaphor for God) be *my* Redeemer? I cannot wait a geological age for salvation. Is God's "eternal changelessness" a source of hope for me, or does it make a mockery of my urgent need, my desperate prayers?[1] Can God's eternity and my frailty ever meet "in real time," as they say? The psalmist has to have an answer to that question, and so he throws the demand in God's face: "The time to have mercy has come!" Israel's peremptory genius for prayer is unparalleled in the history of the world. "You've got to get up! It's past time for *you* to cherish Zion!" (102:14).

And what happens as a result of that urgent prayer for God to act? From one perspective, far too little. The walls of Jerusalem do not rise suddenly out of the rubble. The enemies, the destroyers, do not "get theirs" while our psalmist looks on with satisfaction. Nor does she experience dramatic relief from personal anguish. Only a few verses from the end she is still crying out against God: "Do not take me away half-way through my days; you whose years are from generation to generation!" (102:25). The pastoral value of the laments is that they come from people like the man in the nursing home. People who have experienced irreparable losses—and learned to live with them. People who have hoped for miracles—and not seen them. People who are still waiting for relief, for God's definitive act of deliverance, who are still praying and sometimes cannot remember why. People like some—perhaps many—of us.

In one sense, then, this psalm is a big disappointment. As far as we know, the psalmist never hears God speak; he receives no promise of blessing in abundance, long life, happiness. You will, of course, find such promises in scripture, but rarely in the lament psalms. The laments represent a particular moment in the life of prayer: the moment of radical uncertainty, of terrible fragility. For some, that moment lasts a whole lifetime: for Sudanese Christians who have never known a country without war, for Palestinians who have never known life outside a refugee camp, for a girl living with cancer or a young man with AIDS. This psalm speaks for them: "[God] has stunted my strength in midcourse; he has shortened my days" (102:24). This psalm does for them what promises of long life and abundance could not do. It articulates their experience of God within the canon of scripture. It locates their reality on the map of faith.

So something does happen when the psalmist prays; something changes. What happens is not necessarily the thing we hope for when we pray. We want the situation to get better. But the lament psalms never show us an external improvement *in the situation*. We know such improvement can happen through prayer, and the Bible attests to it, but not in these psalms. They attest to another reality: the change that takes place *in the psalmist* in the act of praying. In a word, the change that takes place here is that our psalmist gains stability. The one who was on the brink of annihilation, discarded by God, who felt insubstantial as smoke, shadow, dried-up grass—now she finds a voice, a standing place in the presence of the God whose years are forever. Praying, the psalmist is able to keep on praying—in this case, for nearly thirty verses. Prayer affords a meeting place between God's eternity and her terrible fragility.

Notably, many of the words of this prayer seem dramatically at odds with the situation. Listen:

> Nations will fear the name of the LORD,
> and all the kings of the earth, your glory.
> For the LORD has built Zion,
> [God] appears in his glory. (102:16-17)

The psalmist is reciting the creed, the confession of ancestral faith. But those words belong to better times than the present. The ancestors watched God build Zion; our psalmist is standing in its rubble. What can their hopelessly outdated words mean to him? Yet the very misfit between the creed and the present situation is what makes this recitation important. It shows us why we recite the creed at all: because ancient faith gives power of resistance against the tyranny of our own immediate experience. Intensely though we feel our experience—and on a Myers-Briggs typology, the lament psalmists are off the scale at the "feeling" end—if we are to endure in faith, then we dare not depend solely on our own experience to tell us who God is, what God is doing, even what God is doing for us. Israel endures as YHWH's people because we are able to lean on the faith of our ancestors, when our own experience will not support us in faith.

This is the difference between biblical faith and paganism: paganism does depend on immediate experience. Worshipers of the god Marduk endured just as long as Marduk's city, Babylon, stood firm; then they disappeared without a living trace. Their prayers, though contemporary with the psalmist's, are known to us solely as archaeological artifacts, like Babylon itself. If Israel had similarly relied upon immediate experience, then its faith and identity would long ago have succumbed to any one of a devastating series of events: Jerusalem destroyed by Babylonians, and later by Romans; the genocidal rampages of Assyrians, later Greeks, later Romans, later Crusaders, later the Tsar, most lately the Nazis.

The church likewise depends upon the confession of faith for its life, from generation to generation, even when that confession seems to contradict our experience of life. Dietrich Bonhoeffer reminded the church of this unsettling truth when he called Christians a people who are identified by their faith, not by their experience, not even their experience of God. Who could rely on their experience in the nightmare years of the Third Reich, when the situation suggested to faithful Jews and Christians that God had abandoned them? Instead, the remnant, the Confessing Church, was thrown back on biblical faith, whose witness to a faithful, merciful, and powerful God we must trust, if we are to endure through the flood tides of history.

> Let this be written for a future generation,
> so that a people yet unborn may praise the LORD—
> that the LORD looks down from his holy height...
> to open a way for those doomed to die. (102:19-21)

"Let this be written for a future generation"—confessing the faith of the ancestors for a generation yet unborn, we may forge a link between God's years that are forever and our own short life span. We confess a faith that is both ancient and future-bound, and doing so we may lose a little of our habitual preoccupation with self, preoccupation that so greatly magnifies our present anxieties and makes our losses loom so large.

Confessing the faith, the psalmist's perspective changes fundamentally. At the end of the prayer, the contrast between God's eternity and the ephemerality of all else we value is still acutely felt. But the contrast is no longer terrible. On the contrary, it now brings assurance:

> [Heaven and earth] will perish, but you will stand.
> Like a garment you will change them, and they
>   shall change.
> But you [God] are the same; your years never end.
> The children of your servants shall abide,
> and their seed in your presence shall endure.
>
> (102:27-29)

"The children of your servants... in your presence shall endure." That is where the psalmist's cry comes to rest, there in God's presence, the terror of personal extinction gone. The servants of God endure through their children, their offspring in faith. Confessing God's holy name from generation to generation in the church gives us stability—not because it affords personal protection against harm, but because it pushes us inexorably toward eternity. Eternity is nothing other than living fully in the presence of God, in this world and the next. Our mortal frailty can never be surmounted in this life—certainly not from our side, and not even from God's. It can only be surrendered into God's service.

Etty Hillesum, a young Dutch Jew who died at Auschwitz, has something to teach us about this. "Surrender," she wrote, "does not mean giving up the ghost, fading away with grief, but offering what little assistance I can wherever it has pleased God to place me."[2] Etty had no illusions about the fate of the Dutch Jews when she wrote those words in her diary. Yet surrendering herself into God's service, she volunteered to go with the first group to be transported to a concentration camp, so she might be where the suffering and fear were worst. "Offering what little assistance I can wherever it has pleased God to place me"—surrendering ourselves in all our frailty into God's hands, thus we enter into

eternity. And there we recognize that our frailty is not meant
to cause us anxiety and sorrow. Rather, God means it to be a
source of confidence, and even, as it was for Etty, a source of
joy. For it is exactly that frailty—the strict limits to our powers, their inevitable failure, the certainty of death—that creates the need and the desire to see God's power at work, in
ourselves, in the church from generation to generation, and
in Christ Jesus for ever and ever—Him in whom frail
humanity and eternal Godhead are fully met and joined,
never to be parted, not even by death on a cross.

Notes

1. A prayer that matches the mood of Psalm 102 reads thus: "Be
present, O merciful God, and protect us through the hours of this
night, so that we who are wearied by the changes and chances of
this life may rest in your eternal changelessness; through Jesus
Christ our Lord" (BCP 133).
2. *An Interrupted Life: The Diaries of Etty Hillesum, 1941-1943*
(New York: Pantheon Books, 1983), 142.

CHAPTER FOURTEEN

VOLUNTARY HEARTBREAK

Psalm 51

PSALM 51 IS THE LENTEN psalm *par excellence,* for it is the only psalm—and perhaps the only passage in the Bible—that offers in-depth guidance for the particular work of that season, the work of contrition. It sounds odd, doesn't it? "Contrition" is an old-fashioned word and a distinctly out-moded concept. Contrition means finding the courage to let your heart break over sin. Willfully letting your heart break and then offering the pieces to God is a radically counter-cultural idea in our society. For the ideal of our time is above all else to be comfortable with ourselves. We have a seeming-ly boundless capacity for self-forgiveness—or better yet, slight inclination to feel guilt in the first place. After all, we're only human, and every one of us, it turns out, is a survivor from a dysfunctional family. Under these circumstances, our goal is psychological ease, not freedom from sin.

This attitude translates into a pastoral style that is often resolutely unchallenging. Some years ago when I was in sem-inary, I was looking for a spiritual director and confessor. I met with a priest and began to lay out for him what our psalmist would accurately call "my transgressions." But soon the young priest fixed me with a kindly, clarifying look and said: "Now, you don't mean to say that you feel guilty about these things." That was, of course, exactly what I meant to say; it was only the intolerable weight of guilt that had moved me to seek a confessor. I believe that the priest was well-intentioned but terribly misguided. Like many other modern Christians, he did not understand that naming our sins before God is a necessary part of the Christian life. Private confession with a priest is helpful to some and not to others, but every Christian needs regularly to get specific about sin, to name her own sins in the presence of God. It is quite simply the only way to get out of the deadly trap laid for us by our sins.

And how does this voluntary heartbreak that we call "contrition" work to free us from sin? The words of a familiar hymn written by Frederick William Faber give us a clue: "There's a wideness in God's mercy, like the wideness of the sea." God's mercy is unimaginably wide—indeed, too wide for us to take in. God's mercy is wide, but our hearts are narrow; they have been constricted by sin. For it is ever the nature of sin to turn us in on ourselves rather than opening us outward toward God and neighbor. God's mercy is wide, but our sin-laden hearts are narrow. The psalmist understands that it is only broken hearts that are truly open toward God:

> Godly sacrifices are a broken spirit;
> a heart broken and crushed, O God, you will not
>   scorn. (51:19)

So we might suppose that God waits to have mercy on us until we are good and devastated by our sins, but the hymn gives us a different picture. God's mercy flows constantly, like the sea, yet much of the time we are simply too hard-hearted to experience it. Contrition enables us to *feel* God's mercy toward us; to speak boldly, it puts God's mercy to work for us. When we let our hearts break before God, the pieces do not sink into oblivion. They are borne up, they float, yes, they sail on the tide of God's mercy. The psalmist knows that, and does not hesitate for a moment in laying claim to the full measure of God's mercy. "Have mercy on me, O God," he cries, "according to your lovingkindness. According to the abundance of your mercy, wipe away my transgressions" (51:3). And his transgressions are horrible: you will remember that this psalm is traditionally spoken by David after his adultery with Bathsheba and the murder of her husband, Uriah. The mercy David demands is measured by his need, not by his deserving. It is measured by God's capacity to love, which is boundless.

So David dares to confess everything, unlike us. We customarily minimize our sins, saying, "Okay, maybe what I did was wrong, but I had a good reason—well, at least a fair excuse." But David *maximizes* his sins, confessing far more than any reasonable person would: "Look, I was born with iniquity; and in sin my mother conceived me" (51: 7). "I was born with iniquity"—can you hear how radical is that statement, cutting through all the sentimentality that we customarily attach to a new life? "In sin my mother conceived me"—but we miss the point if we hear this as the expression of a festering psychological wound. Rather, the psalmist is confronting us with a truth about human life that we almost never acknowledge: every newborn child enters into a web of human relations that is already deeply flawed. We are born morally compromised; the slate is never blank for any of us. By reason of race, gender, social location, our particular parentage, even our individual biological makeup, we were (you might say) "set up" to hurt others and to be hurt by them. That is part of what it means to speak of original sin, a theological notion that has fallen out of fashion but is in fact indispensable to understanding both our guilt and our suffering.

"In sin my mother conceived me." We rebel against this idea; naturally, we wish to be free from any involvement in the sins of others, to have a straight shot at righteousness. The desire is natural enough, but nonetheless it is an inhuman desire. For if it were possible not to be involved in the sins of others, then we would be living in this world without any history. So this is how the Christian faith tells our history. Along with the physical and temperamental characteristics I have from my parents, I also inherited a propensity for sin, for preferring to seek my own way rather than waiting for God's way to be revealed. That impatient self-seeking is, of course, the original sin committed by Eve and Adam in the Garden of Eden, and it has been committed by every human being since, except for One. In a more personal way, also, I am involved in my parents' sins. Many of my particular sins are rooted in fears and resentments I picked up from them, and they from their parents. I am thoughtless in many of the same ways they are thoughtless. "I was born with iniquity."

171

Our inherited sins are not only familial but social as well. Being a North American at this stage in the world's history means that each of us participates more or less actively in a culture whose abiding sin is massive waste. Each year we discard enough solid waste to build a wall along the U. S.–Canadian border that is two hundred feet high and seventy-five feet wide; that imaginary wall stands as a monument to our greed and heedlessness of the generations that will come after us.

We are born into sin. That is the psalmist's first radical insight. Joined with that is the insight, no less radical, that all our sin is aimed against God:

172

> Against you—you only—I have sinned
> and I have done what is evil in your sight. (51: 6)

Few of us, I think, ever imagine that our sin hurts God most of all. We think chiefly of the human consequences. Certainly Uriah suffered permanent damage from David's sin. Yet David says, "Against you [God]—you only—I have sinned." In his contrition David moves to a deeper level of reality; he sees what is in fact the deepest truth of biblical faith, the truth that underlies the whole story from the Garden of Eden to Golgotha. The truth is this: God is terribly vulnerable to human sin. Our sin is more than an affront to God's justice. It is a tearing pain in God's heart and God's gut.

What we must face is the fact that God's vulnerability to sin is total, even unto death on a cross. That is what it means to say that God is love. For every human lover knows that the downside of love is vulnerability to pain. Therefore perfect love is at the same time perfect vulnerability. The message of the cross is that God's love is indeed powerful to overcome sin, but Love conquers only by relaxing all defenses against sin. Christ conquers only by receiving all the wounds sin has to inflict.

David knows God's terrible vulnerability to our sin. And he responds with his own total vulnerability. He owns up to his sin without excuse, without appeal to extenuating circumstances:

> For my transgressions I know,
> and my sin is ever before me. (51:5)

Now we can see why David is called "a man after God's heart" (1 Samuel 13:14). David is truly after God's heart and does not stop until he feels in his own heart what is there. He does not stop even when he feels the sharpest pain it is possible for anyone to feel, and which perhaps only a few saints feel fully: the pain of seeing our sins exactly as God must see them. That divine pain is literally unbearable for a human being, and it breaks David's heart:

173

> The sacrifice acceptable to God is a broken spirit;
> a heart broken and crushed, O God, you will not
>   scorn. (51:19)

We would prefer it another way, and even now we can convince ourselves that David has got it wrong. After all, one might reason, a spirit that had once been badly broken is a fragile instrument for God's service. Better, we think, to retain our resiliency, to bounce back even from the worst of our sins, to look forward and not back! But David is past that kind of self-serving logic—past it in desperation, and past it also in faith. When our heart has truly been crushed by sin, we do not bounce back. We cry out: "Create for me a clean heart, O God." Three times in our psalm, in three successive verses, David pleads for a new spirit, pleads that God's Spirit may enter where his own spirit has been crushed: "Renew a right spirit within me.... Do not take your holy Spirit from me.... Sustain me with your bountiful Spirit" (51:12-14).

In his desperation, David's instinct for the ways of God is unerring. He is seeking forgiveness: "Wipe away all my iniquities" (51:11). And the sustained pleas for God's holy Spirit show that David knows exactly what forgiveness is. It is not, as we commonly think, something God *does*, to us or for us, taking away our spots like a sort of metaphysical dry-cleaner. Rather, forgiveness is God's immediate presence with us in our sin. It is God's holy Spirit rushing to the place that opens when our spirit breaks. Forgiveness is God's generous Spirit poured out upon the dry bones of Ezekiel's great vision (Ezekiel 37:1-14), soaking them, restoring wholeness and strength to serve. Forgiveness is God's very presence with us, and for many of us our first deep experience of that comes in exactly this moment out of which David now prays: the moment of contrition, when, having exhausted all strategies for evading or excusing our sin, we are driven to acknowledge that, like God, we are terribly wounded by it. And the scarcely believable good news of our psalm is this: the moment of contrition is also the moment of forgiveness, when God's Spirit—which is all generosity, all love outpoured—meets our spirit, which is all thirsting need.

Yes, but how can we keep from deceiving ourselves? Can we ever really know that we have been forgiven? How can we know for sure that God's bountiful Spirit has met and healed our broken spirit? The answer is surprisingly simple: we will know when our prayer changes. Brokenhearted David prays:

O Lord open my lips,
and my mouth will proclaim your praise. (51:17)

When we find ourselves (contrary to our own expectation) singing God's praise, then we will know that forgiveness has happened. For the freedom to praise God is the measure of our freedom from sin.

This is the essential dynamic of the kingdom of heaven: lamenting our sins, we find ourselves suddenly praising God. That is how all of us must draw close to God. Probably no Christian has represented that dynamic more vividly than Dante, when he envisions Christians climbing up the mountain of Purgatory toward God. Dante's Purgatory is not just a medieval fantasy of what happens when you die; it is a penetrating vision of what the church looks like even now—or should look like, if indeed it is helping us get free from our sins. The climb up the mountain of Purgatory is difficult. For all God's mercy, it is still slow, painstaking work, both owning our sins and leaving them behind, for we have grown so attached to them. The climb up the mountain is difficult, yet Dante's Purgatory is not a grim place—far from it. For the laboring souls are all the while singing hymns to encourage one another, shouting out the praises of the God to whom they are journeying, the God who is in fact already with them in Purgatory, for it is God's bountiful Spirit that sustains them on the way.

Chapter Fifteen

SERVING IN THE SHADOWS

Isaiah 49

The LORD made my mouth like a sharp sword;
  in the shadow of his hand he hid me.
And he made me as a polished arrow;
  in his quiver he concealed me. (Isaiah 49:2)

I DARESAY THESE are not the images we normally remember from the short poem that biblical scholars call the Second Servant Song of Isaiah. The famous image comes a few verses later:

I will give you as a light to the nations,
  that my salvation may be to the end of the earth.
                                              (49:6)

Unstoppable light, spreading salvation. Christians have, of course, seen in this compelling metaphor a promise fulfilled in Jesus Christ, the light of the world. It is further fulfilled in the mission and ministry of the church: Christians go forth "in the power of the Spirit," "to love and serve the Lord."

Such an image can encourage the church as it turns from the inwardness of Lent to the bright Easter hope that begs to be shared. For those who have chosen to live as Christians, choosing that option over the more immediately attractive alternatives our culture offers, this image of light may recall what drew them to the church in the first place: the desire to do something significant in the world, even something good for the world, that theologians call "a sense of mission."

Yet we may be misled about the nature of Christian mission and ministry if we fail to note that the poem does not begin with spreading light, but with the very opposite, with images of concealment. The model servant is a sharp sword hidden in the shadow of God's hand, a polished arrow tucked into God's quiver. The direction of the poem suggests that this is where power for ministry is generated: in the hidden place. We must first inhabit these images of concealment if, through us, God is one day to realize the goal of spreading light. The prophetic poem suggests to us the necessity of practicing a discipline of obscurity—a countercultural practice if ever there was one, and therefore most appropriate for us to consider as we practice walking the way of the cross.

Living in the deep shadow of God's hand, hiding in the quiver that rides on God's back—thus the great poet we call the Second Isaiah reminds us that the servant's preparation for effective public ministry occurs in out-of-the-way places, where perhaps no one much notices, approves of, or is grateful for what we do. It is the hidden places where we are most closely under God's protective care. This is a truth easily forgotten in the environments most of us inhabit, where many people aspire to a few obviously desirable positions, and disappointment is a regular experience. Yet the very existence of this second part of the book of Isaiah[1] challenges our common assumption that public recognition is the standard of success in the Christian life, as it is taken to be in other walks of life. For the sublime poetry of these sixteen chapters is itself the fruit of a hard discipline of obscurity. The prophet-poet's real name was perhaps never known or was forgotten millennia ago. And more, the so-called Second Isaiah speaks to and for a people thrown into exile, the ultimate out-of-the-way place. From Babylon, the rubbish heap of nations, it seemed most unlikely that any light would ever shine.

It is because we so much need obscurity and often do not know how to value it that the scriptures repeatedly remind us of that need. Listen to the psalmists:

> Keep us, O LORD, as the apple of your eye;
> hide us under the shadow of your wings.
>
> (Psalm 17:8)

> For you have been my help,
> and in the shadow of your wings I will sing for joy.
>
> (Psalm 63:7)

> Be to me a rocky refuge to enter into always,
>   to save me;
> for you are my rock and my fortress. (Psalm 71:3)

Likewise, Jesus knew that God's presence is most palpable in the out-of-the-way places. That is why, in need of new strength, he often went off by himself, *kat 'idian.* Jesus withdrew "to a deserted place by himself" (Matthew 14:13, 23) to absorb the shocking news that his cousin John had been beheaded. *Kat 'idian,* off by himself, he reckoned with the loss of the one who had understood him best. Withdrawn in prayer, he gathered strength to face the approach of his own violent death.[2] Jesus taught his disciples, too, to practice the discipline of obscurity: to find strength, to find God in the hidden place. When the disciples returned from that first great mission of preaching and healing, Jesus did not say,

"We're on a roll!"—and begin strategizing the next great evangelical thrust. Rather he said, "Come away to a deserted place all by yourselves [*kat 'idian*] to rest for a while" (Mark 6:31; compare Luke 9:10).

179

Seeking refuge and rest in the hidden place is, or should be, an essential discipline of the Christian life, and for this reason: there is a war going on here, and we are involved in it. The Bible is an extended work of military history, chronicling God's battle against evil from the third chapter of Genesis right through the book of Revelation. What the exilic poet tells us is that *we* are God's weapons of war; the servants of God are sharpened swords and polished arrows to be used against evil. Now, this is a hard idea for us modern Christians to grasp. We do not talk much about evil, and we certainly do not style ourselves as faith warriors. But the biblical poet presses us to face what is really going on here, week after week, when we come to worship; or day after day, when we read scripture and pray in our own rooms; or when we meet with other Christians to talk about what we believe and are struggling to make real in our lives, sometimes against sizable odds. Each of those activities may have some place, large or small, in the lives of each of us; all of them are the means by which we are being sharpened and polished to recognize and name evil, to be useful to God in fighting against all the forms of evil that we live with every single day.

But here is where things get complicated. For of course we do not fight the battle against evil as outsiders: none of us is personally immune to evil. And so if we are to be useful in God's service, then we must often pull out of the action and clarify our own position. We must go to a place apart—even if, like Israel in exile, we enter it against our will and with much suffering—in order that we may see the evil clearly and understand our own ready complicity in it.

The early Christians knew well that even with the best intentions and the brightest hopes we easily fall captive to the powers that destroy life. Therefore they practiced what they called the *disciplina arcana,* the secret discipline. They engaged in studied reflection on the mysteries by which we live: the mystery of sin that reaches into every corner of God's created world, and of redemption that does the same; of divine humility so profound that once cosmic majesty stooped to take on the life of a Galilean peasant; of divine power that hid itself deep in human frailty and submitted even to death on a cross. As the first Christians knew, whenever the church finds itself living and speaking in ways that too much resemble the dominant culture, then it is time to exercise the *disciplina arcana* with renewed rigor. In other words, whenever the church gets too comfortable, then it is time to sacrifice our culturally acceptable eloquence and dwell on those mysteries that we can comprehend and express only haltingly.

Like Israel in exile, we all live in constant danger of assimilating to the ways and wisdom of the various empires where we dwell. These may be of great value in themselves. My own Babylon is a thriving university, a place where I am glad to be. But it becomes dangerous to me when I look to its professional agenda to shape my ministry of teaching and aim at the rewards it offers. The danger of assimilating is for all of us acute, and possibly greatest for those parishes and individuals who enjoy what we call "successful ministries." Therefore we must continually interrupt our progress and return time and again to the secret place where we live closely with those mysteries—in minutes jealously guarded for private prayer, in hours each week or month reserved for spiritual reading and study, in days set aside for retreats.

It is not only because of the danger of assimilation that we must constantly seek the hidden place. It is also, and even more, because the battle against evil is bloody and deeply sad, and anyone who has the courage to stay in it will feel like she is losing most of the time. Modern psychology did not discover the twin phenomena of despair and burnout that afflict so many people who want most of all to serve God. The poet of the Babylonian exile saw both the problem and its only remedy, which lies precisely in the practice of taking refuge in God:

And I said, "In vain have I labored;
for waste and absurdity have I spent my strength."
Ah, but my cause is with YHWH,
And my recompense with my God. (49:4)

"My cause is with YHWH"—that is an expression of nearly blind trust. If we would serve God at all, then we must be content to do it blind, for there is very little light at the bottom of the quiver. Serving God truly means moving forward guided only by trust and the instinct of faith—the well-honed instinct that keeps us close to God in the darkness, that holds us steady and does not deteriorate into calculation about any satisfying result we might see from our labors. Being wholly free to serve means allowing our cause to rest with God, content in this world to work and love and wait and pray with the strength that is given us, even though we are unable to envision any bright outcome.

The freedom to do that comes from reflecting on what happened to us at the baptismal font, where we were plunged deep into God's quiver, our "life hidden with Christ in God" (Colossians 3:3). Because our life is now securely hidden in God, we can relax in God's service. We are free to serve God with whatever skills we have. And when those skills fail (as they will), then we may go on serving through our willingness to share God's own abiding grief and endless love for the world. Through baptism our life is hidden with Christ in

182

God, and so while we are in this world we are wise to plunge often and deep into obscurity, where God's protective presence is most palpable. We must choose solitude often. This will strengthen us to accept the obscurity we did not choose, when, like our prophet, we are sent into exile—and we will all go there, at one time or another. Then we must find our faith and our ministry in the place of loneliness, of no vision; in the hidden place despised by the world yet made habitable for us through God's stupendous humility in Jesus Christ our Lord, with whom we find our only rest, through whom we offer all our praise.

Notes

1. Chapters 40-55 are generally considered to come, not from Isaiah of Jerusalem (the eighth-century prophet whose message and history are preserved in the first 39 chapters), but from an anonymous sixth-century poet, whom scholars call "the Second Isaiah."

2. See Matthew 16:21.

PART FIVE

TORAH OF THE EARTH

IN THIS PART we will focus on a contemporary issue, the ecological crisis, which may be the most far-reaching *theological* crisis (for it is that) ever to confront the church. It is a surprising fact, unsuspected even among Christians who now recognize the depth and dimensions of the crisis, that the Old Testament is the most valuable resource we have for formulating our own response. But how can that be, since the biblical writers knew nothing of our looming disaster? The answer is that they were pervasively aware that God is Creator of everything that is. We might think that the biblical story of creation ends with the first chapter of Genesis, but in fact it continues through Torah, Prophets, Proverbs, and Psalms. With a subtle understanding that grows more impressive as our own theological and ecological awareness deepens, the biblical writers explore the infinitely complex web of relationships, with the earth and the non-human creatures, in which we are embedded. Further, they help us see the degree to which our relationship with God is bound up in our relationships with the other creatures whom God has made. It is the consistent witness of the Bible that disorder or heedlessness in one area is *invariably* reflected in the other. Conversely, reverence for the earth and reverence for God cannot be separated. The fertile earth is the best assurance of God's generosity toward humankind. At the same time its fruitful yet fragile beauty constitutes an ongoing call to responsibility and, for many of us, repentance and change of life.

184

CHAPTER SIXTEEN

"GOOD-FAITH SPRINGS UP FROM THE EARTH"

Learning Ecology From the Bible

AT FIRST BLUSH, the concept of "biblical ecology" seems to be an oxymoron—like "jumbo shrimp." Ecology as a specialized academic subject, a "science," is barely a couple of generations old, and the ecological crisis we now face is largely a by-product of technological changes that have taken place in the last two hundred years. The Bible comes from a primarily agrarian society that would have been puzzled by our academic specializations and compartmentalizations. Nonetheless, I think it is no exaggeration to say that the Bible can teach us or (better, perhaps) help us to understand all the fundamentals of ecology. The Bible can enable us to grasp the depth dimensions of the ecological crisis because the ecological crisis is essentially not a technological crisis, but a theological one. It is a massive disordering in our relationship with God, the Creator of heaven and earth.

Ecology, then, is a distinctly theological subject, even a distinctly Old Testament subject. The word ecology literally means "the study of relationships," and it is a striking fact that the Old Testament is pervasively interested in the relationships that obtain between humanity and the nonhuman creation—most especially, our relationship with the fertile soil. As we shall see, the health (or the dis-ease) of that relationship is viewed as a primary index of the health of the relationship between humanity and God. Therefore, one of the surprises in store for contemporary readers of the Bible is the depth of insight into our present situation that the Old Testament consistently offers.

I read the Old Testament in order to grasp the depth dimension, that is, the genuinely theological dimension of the ecological crisis, and to look for guidance in moving beyond it. This is not to say that the Old Testament is an early ecological tract. Out of necessity, the ancient Israelites were indeed what we would call "ecologically sensitive": the highlands and deserts of Israel constituted one of the most fragile of the habitable zones on the planet, and the most essential resources of soil and water stood always in danger of depletion. But I do not wish to collapse the historical distance between ancient Israel's situation and our own experience of widespread degradation of the planet as a result of advanced technologies and modern population growth. The biblical writers neither knew firsthand our planet's great distress, nor did they mystically foresee it.

Yet even if the Bible is not in this sense "prophetic" about the modern situation, that word may still suggest how it provides guidance for us who are in acute crisis. For what all true prophets do is help us to see our situation as it really is. They let us catch a glimpse of our hearts and our actions as God must view them—and, if we are wise, we will render our own judgment on them. In various ways, all the biblical prophets call us to "righteousness" (Hebrew *tsedek, tsedaqah*) in relationships with God and neighbor. Righteousness is not a static condition, attainable by following a fixed set of prescriptions. Rather, it is a quality of wholeness in all our relationships. Of course, we never achieve such integrity once and for all; at best, we are always "pursuing" righteousness, as the prophetic preacher of Deuteronomy (16:20) puts it.

In our present situation, the Bible's prophetic word to us may be that the most pivotal of all our neighborly relations is one we hardly consider at all, namely our relationship with the fertile soil. The disorienting and reorienting message of the Bible is, simply stated: *Righteousness means living in humble, care-full, and godly relationship with the soil on which the life of every one of us wholly depends.* This view of righteousness is considerably different from—and probably more than—what modern churchgoers (urbanites and suburbanites as most of us are) think we have signed on for. Hearing and accepting it necessitates a hard look at the biblical text from a new perspective. Finally, it necessitates what the New Testament writers call *metanoia*, literally "a change of mind," the radical shift of mindset that we call "repentance."

A first step toward ecological repentance is the recognition that the Bible does not confine the operation of righteousness to the human sphere, as we generally do. When the biblical poets open up their imaginations to envision righteousness in full bloom, this is the kind of thing they see:

Ahhh, [God's] saving-grace is close to those who
    fear him,
so that glory may dwell on our earth.
Covenant-loyalty and good-faith meet one another,
righteousness and wellbeing [*shalom*] kiss.
Good-faith springs up from the earth,
and righteousness peers out of the heavens.
Yes, YHWH will give what is good,
and our earth will give its full-yield.
Righteousness will go before him
and make a path for his steps. (Psalm 85:10-14)

188

Here the psalmist casts a net so wide that we can scarcely comprehend how she holds these ideas together. What possible connection could there be between human fear of God and the earth giving a good crop? Is "good-faith springs up from the earth" anything more than a metaphor that once strayed across a poet's mind and somehow got immortalized as scripture? In order to begin to answer those questions, we need to go back to the vision of what we might call "original righteousness," the picture of the first human beings at the moment when God formed them and gave them their own special place in the web of life.

A Healthy Materiality

As is well known, modern biblical scholarship has identified two originally separate creation accounts that have been fused in the first two chapters of Genesis. They apparently come from two writers, working perhaps several centuries apart, who differ considerably in their interests and literary styles. Of particular interest to us are the distinct ways each of them characterizes the newly created human being. For the writer of the first chapter, known as "the Priestly Source," the salient fact, repeated three times, is that humanity—both male and female—is created "in the image of God" (Genesis 1:26, 27). Their exalted vocation is to "exercise dominion" over the other creatures and even to "conquer the earth (or: land; Hebrew *'eretz*)"—the identical charge given to the Israelites poised at the edge of the Promised Land. In both cases, human beings are given the weighty honor and responsibility of representing God's benevolent dominion in the world, of standing up for God's interests in the face of every threat. They are to stand for God even against the threat of their own short-sighted self-interest. (The long story of the Bible will demonstrate that the unenlightened self-interest of those whom God has chosen for special responsibility is by far the greatest challenge to God's sovereignty.)

The second writer, known as "the Yahwist,"[1] sees a very different derivation: "And YHWH God formed the human being [*'adam*], dust from the fertile soil [*'adamah*]..." (2:7). This is a rare instance where Hebrew wordplay can be captured well in English: humans come from humus. In this account, the vocation of humanity is to get their hands dirty: "And YHWH God took the human being and set 'him' in the Garden of Eden to work it and to watch it" (2:15).

Unquestionably, the editors who fused the two creation accounts intended us to see them as complementary components of a single story. Together, the two images give us a rich understanding of the derivation and the destiny of the human being: we are connected on one side of the family with divinity; on the other, with the fertile soil. To use a phrase from the African-American tradition, we might say that the first chapter of Genesis gives us a sense of "somebodyness." We are made in the image of God; we have infinite worth and a high destiny. But the second creation account implicitly warns us not to get a distorted opinion of ourselves. The Yahwist advises that the humus has left an indelible imprint on every human being: "For dust you are, and to dust you shall return" (3:19). In the context of the biblical narrative, that reminder is God's counter to the attractive but deadly delusion encouraged by the snake, of power exercised without limit. The snake enticed the humans to imagine themselves becoming "like gods, knowing good and bad" (3:5). God pops that bubble and introduces them to the difficult concept of their own finitude: dust to dust.

The two biblical symbols—humanity made in the image of God and human from humus—belong together, but in practice most contemporary Christians separate them. I think it is fair to say that our self-estimation generally owes more to the first chapter of the Bible than to the second. We rightly remember that we have something of God in us, but we tend to forget the equal claim that the soil lays upon us. For us in this generation, the call to discipleship may well be a call to remember our kinship with the fertile earth. If we are listening to the Bible's prophetic witness to the present rapacious age, then we should be as shocked and radically reoriented as were those (few, perhaps) who heard and heeded Amos or Jeremiah, when we are told that the soil is more like a relative than a resource: it is to be respected, and not just used. For us, heeding the prophetic call means turning away from the rampant materialism that infects our society to the *healthy materiality* that is the first principle of a biblical ecology.

Every Ash Wednesday, Christians participate in an exercise in healthy materiality. "Remember that you are dust, and to dust you shall return," the priest recites (BCP 265). This rehearsal of the second creation account warns us against an over-spiritualized understanding of our discipleship; the dusty cross on our foreheads signals where our "spiritual journey" is headed. In the traditional language of Christian monasticism, living in holy awareness of our mortality is known as "mortifying the flesh." Mortification literally means "making death." Some monastics have given the practice a bad name, taking it as an occasion to abuse their bodies with whips or excessive fasting.

But there is a completely different way of understanding mortification. One contemporary monk defines mortification as "the decision to live a simple life of moderation as much in tune with the dignity of life as is possible."[2] By this definition, mortification is the furthest thing from a tortuous denial of our physical being. Rather, "making death" means acknowledging in all our ways that we are dustbound creatures. Although our existence is finite, we are privileged to extend the significance of our lives beyond the confines of our own egos. This is possible through the divine gift of community. And the way we join in community with the other creatures with whom we share this earth, now and after our own death, is by limiting our own consumption in order to honor the dignity of *all* life. Mortification is, then, one traditional name for the way of living and thinking that I am calling "healthy materiality." It is the exact opposite of the attitude that finds popular expression in the bumper sticker, "Whoever has the most stuff when they die wins."

Torah of the Earth
The link between humans and humus represents more than family history. As the biblical writer we call "the Yahwist" understands it, the link also bespeaks vocation: "And YHWH God took the human being and set 'him' in the Garden of Eden to work it and to watch it" (2:15). It would be easy enough to explain this first biblical reference to human work as no more than what one would expect from ancient Israelites. They were, most of them, farmers; how else would they reconstruct the first human job description? But close examination shows that this statement is more than a cultural—or agricultural—commonplace. The Yahwist has chosen words carefully, and made some unexpected choices. When those words are probed, they reveal a profound and far-reaching statement of the relationship that God wills to obtain between humanity and the fertile soil on which the life of every person depends. The biblical writer is giving us a glimpse of "original righteousness," the divinely desired state of relationship that, we might imagine, existed for the shimmering moment before human disobedience threw things out of kilter.

Neither of the key verbs designating human activity in the garden belongs primarily to the Hebrew vocabulary of horticulture or agriculture. The standard translation—"to till it and tend it"[3]—is therefore somewhat misleading. Each of these words, which I have provisionally translated as "work" (*'avad*) and "watch" (*shamar*), occurs hundreds of times throughout the Old Testament, and in only a tiny fraction of those occurrences do they have anything to do with working the soil. What they do frequently designate is human activity directed toward God, and we might guess that the Yahwist chose them precisely for their strong religious resonance. The word *'avad* means "to work" but also "to work for" someone. In the context of ancient societies, it denotes a slave's or a servant's service to a master, either human or divine. And the Supreme Master in the Bible is, of course, God. Thus YHWH repeatedly challenges Pharaoh the slave-master to release the Israelites to an alternative form of nonelective service: "Let my people go, that they may *'avad* me!" (Exodus 8:1, 20; 9:1, 13). When *'avad* is directed toward God, it means "worship." Even stronger are the religious connotations of the second verb, *shamar* ("to watch" or "watch over," "observe," "keep" or "preserve"). In the vast majority of occurrences of this verb, the thing that is to be "observed" is God's Torah: "You shall *shamar* my commandment, ordinance, covenant, Sabbath" (for example, Exodus 13:10, 20:6, 31:14). Thus Israel is repeatedly charged to keep on the watch against violation, distortion, or simple forgetfulness of the divine Teaching on which its life depends.

The philological details are important. Taken together, these two resonant verbs give depth and precision to our understanding of the kind of relationship that God first envisioned between the human creatures and the soil from which they were taken. And if we are surprised by the understandings they yield, then that is the Bible's prophetic function at work. When familiar relationships are suddenly seen from a wholly new perspective—seen as God might see them—then we are being prophetically disoriented and at the same time reoriented toward Torah's urgent commandment: "Righteousness, righteousness you must pursue" (Deuteronomy 16:20).

The first reorienting idea, stemming from the verb *'avad,* is that the land is something we may be expected to serve. Typically we think of fertile soil as a "natural resource." But the Bible has chosen a verb which implies that we are to see ourselves in a relation of *subordination* to the land on which we live. Recognizing the metaphor of servitude implicit in this first job description, we can say that the biblical writer— or, to use a more traditional and still valid concept about biblical authorship, the Holy Spirit—envisions humans habitually deferring to the soil. The needs of the land take clear precedence over our own immediate preferences, as the master's requirements override a servant's desires. The Bible's prophetic speech is typically not only startling, but also realistic. For in plain fact, we humans are dependents living in the household of which the fertile earth is the head. It is the soil that determines how the household economy runs. We are something like household retainers—rendering useful service, but nonetheless remaining in dependent relationship. We need the food, clothing, and shelter that are guaranteed only by the prosperity and good favor of the head of the household.

The second verb, *shamar,* suggests the metaphor of legal observance: the charge to keep the fertile soil is akin to the familiar charge to keep God's Torah and commandments. This metaphor is as unexpected as that of servitude. It implies something most of us have never considered: there are divinely established rules and constraints attached to our use of the soil, and it has always been so. "Observe it"—learn from it and about it; "keep it"—from harm and violation. Thus the word *shamar* suggests that, even under the ideal

193

conditions of Eden, humans were laboring under God's Torah of the soil. Far from inventing our relationship to the land, our task has always been (in the words of one modern agrarian thinker) "meeting the expectations of the land."[4]

194

Alongside the metaphorical meaning of legal observance, the verb *shamar* has a second common meaning that is important for our understanding of our relationship to the soil. Often *shamar* denotes the act of watchful protection. Thus the psalmist frequently appeals to God:

> Watch over [*shamar*] me, God, for I have taken
> refuge in you. (Psalm 16:1)

> Keep [*shamar*] me as the apple of your eye.
> (Psalm 17:8)

> Preserve [*shamar*] my life, for I am faithful.
> Save your servant—you, God!—the one who is
> trusting in you! (Psalm 86:2)

For the person who is vulnerable, God's acts of watching over, keeping, and preserving are the substance of covenant relationship. Reciprocally, Torah and Prophets repeatedly call on Israel to protect weak members of the covenant community: the widow, the orphan, and the sojourner. The charge in Genesis to keep the land can be heard as an extension of that prophetic concern for the vulnerable, expanding the sphere of covenant obligation to include the soil itself.[5]

Together, these two verbs outline humanity's complex relationship with the fertile soil, a relationship that is meant to be deferential, observant, and protective. We must serve (*'avad*) the land, not worshipping it but showing it reverence as God's own creation[6], respecting it as one whose needs take priority over our immediate desires. We must watch it and watch over it (*shamar*) as one who has something to teach us and yet at the same time needs our vigilant care. The religiously resonant language of this first job description from Eden suggests the remarkable teaching that in showing proper regard for the fertile earth, we meet the two great goals of all Torah observance: serving God and protecting the weak. This indeed is Torah of the earth.

Good-Faith Eating
This biblical picture of right relationship between humanity and the soil should disturb us, for it gives the lie to an idea now well established in our culture. The dominant practices of modern industrial agriculture are based on the idea that technology has given us the power to reinvent our human relationship to the soil. So this is the idea by which most of us are now eating. But it is a dangerous idea:

> For a long time now we have understood ourselves as traveling toward some sort of industrial paradise, some new Eden conceived and constructed entirely by human ingenuity. And we have thought ourselves free to use and abuse nature in any way that might further this enterprise. Now we face overwhelming evidence that we are not smart enough to recover Eden by assault, and that nature does not tolerate or excuse our abuses. If, in spite of the evidence against us, we are finding it hard to relinquish our old ambition, we are also seeing more clearly every day how that ambition has reduced or enslaved us. *We see how everything— the whole world—is belittled by the idea that all creation is moving or ought to move toward an end that some body, some human body, has thought up.* To be free of that end and that ambition would be a delightful and precious thing. Once free of it, we might again go about our work and our lives with a seriousness and a pleasure denied to us when we merely submit to a fate

already determined by gigantic politics, economics, and technology.[7]

Wendell Berry—poet, essayist, and novelist—is perhaps the most articulate spokesman for the perspective of modern agrarianism. The vision of people living in a permanent committed relationship with nature, a relationship of dependence on and responsibility to the fertile soil, is what animates the agrarian movement. In steadily growing numbers, farmers and non-farmers are identifying with that vision. In doing so, they are consciously setting themselves against the social and "natural" disaster now looming in the form of the apparently boom-business of corporate-owned agriculture. Agrarians are calling this generation to reckon with the fact that we are currently buying cheap food at the cost of the long-term health of our soil and water. Aquifers and rivers are over-pumped or polluted by chemical run-off. Hog factories produce "natural fertilizer" in such quantities that lakes and streams become uninhabitable for fish, and rural neighborhoods for people. Erosion rates soar as forests and other kinds of natural covering are removed and more marginal land is plowed. Agrarians bring us the prophetic message that there is a time limit set for the exercise of folly, "that nature does not tolerate or excuse our abuses."

Consciously or not, the agrarians are bringing us a message that is genuinely prophetic—that is, it accords with what we may understand from the Bible about the function of prophecy. In a nontechnical but nonetheless authentic sense, it qualifies as prophecy on three grounds. First, what agrarians tell us about how we stand in relation to the fertile earth conforms on all essential points to the picture set forth in scripture. Serving and preserving the land, observing its natural limits, and protecting it from violation—all these are the basic operating principles of modern agrarianism. Although agrarians are more likely to be organic farmers than preachers, they often talk in terms congenial with those of the biblical writers: "We are living from mystery, from creatures we did not make and powers we cannot comprehend."[8] An agrarian would comprehend these lines from Job more readily and deeply than the average biblical scholar:

197

> Ask now the beasts, and they will teach you;
> and the birds of the heavens, and they will declare
>   to you.
> Or converse with the earth, and it will teach you:
> and the fishes of the sea will recount to you.
> Who among all these does not know
> that the hand of YHWH has done this—
> in whose hand is the life of every creature?
>
> (Job 12:7-10)

Second, the agrarian movement qualifies as prophetic because, like the biblical prophets, agrarians are issuing a fundamental challenge to power. They expose the self-serving "wisdom" promoted by the multinational conglomerates that control the vast majority of food production and processing in this country. The stated goal of feeding the world glosses over a policy of securing maximum profit for corporations and their stockholders, whatever the cost to farmers, the land, and the heritage—of both genetic material and human knowledge—available to future generations of farmers. In industrialized nations, the seed base for many crops has been effectively reduced to a few hybrids that are chemically dependent and require extensive irrigation. In the Third World, rain forests are leveled to raise export crops and satisfy our appetite for coffee and beef. Probably the most essential "natural resource" now being lost is farmers themselves. As agribusiness booms, small farmers in this country and abroad are going under at an unprecedented rate. The American Midwest is now dotted with twentieth-century ghost-towns; there are more prisoners in this country than farmers. And when the farmers disappear from the land their families have tended for generations, so does the knowledge and the caring that preserve its long-term health and productivity. Against the food industry's single-minded insistence on profitability, the agrarians forcefully assert the goal of permanence. They are concerned to leave a rich inheritance for coming generations. In other words, they practice what the monastics call mortification: they live in healthy and humble awareness of their own death, and they desire to leave something good to be remembered by.

Third, the agrarian movement qualifies as prophetic in that it speaks for what we might call the interest of God—that is, the true interest of all people over many generations. Like the biblical prophets, the agrarians confront us with ancient and indispensable insight that is now in danger of being lost, with terrible consequences for this and future generations. Their insight is that not one of us can escape our dependence on the soil and our responsibility to it. That responsibility is shared by everyone who eats. Even if we live in the city and never set foot on a farm, agrarians remind us that we are negotiating our relationship to the soil every day of our lives, with every trip to the grocery store, every meal we cook or microwave or take out. We are negotiating the relationship between human and humus each time we decide (consciously or, more likely, unconsciously) whether to put the vegetable peels down the garbage disposal or in the compost bin.

In a word, agrarianism calls us to pay attention to the fact that eating is the act that embeds us most fully in creation, for better, for worse. Through it we may enact our faith that food is in reality not a commodity on the stock exchange but a gift from God. There is nothing new about that insight. It is as old as prophetic faith itself. Equally, there is nothing new about mistaking the gift for a commodity. Already in the eighth century B.C.E., the prophet Hosea castigated Israel for completely missing the source of her agricultural wealth. Israelites were worshipping one or another local fertility god, whose generic name is Baal, using cultic sex in order to curry divine favor, and thus (they imagined) secure the food supply. Hosea enables us to hear YHWH's anguish at Israel's perverse faith:

> And she did not know
> that it was I, I who gave her
> the grain and the new wine and the oil...
> She said, "They are a present to me,
> which my lovers gave me...."
> And she went after her lovers—
> but me she forgot! says YHWH. (Hosea 2:10, 14, 15)

Hosea's metaphor of harlotry makes the point that Israel is looking for agricultural "presents" from her sugar-daddy gods without taking on the demands of covenant relationship. And, stretching our capacity for cultural criticism over nearly three millennia, we can see that while the form of bad faith has changed, its substance is remarkably stable. For the Baal cult and the food-and-farming industry have this is common: they are seeking thrills without regard for the consequences. Inducing fertility by ritual sex or massive doses of chemical fertilizer and modified genes—these practices express ancient and modern failures to understand that we eat only in the context of covenant community, that is, in the context of long-term and inalienable responsibility both to God and to the soil that God has given us to "work and to watch."

The prophetic message for us is that we eat either in good faith or in bad; "good-faith springs up from the earth." For those of us who are not farmers, perhaps the first step to good-faith eating is learning something about where our food comes from, and what is the real cost—to soil and water sources—of growing or raising it. What will our great-grandchildren have to pay for our cheap food? A second step is caring enough to make changes in our habits of buying and eating—for example, buying food from the community-supported agriculture networks that have sprung up around many urban areas, or buying local (and often endangered) varieties of apples and tomatoes at the farmer's market instead of commercial hybrids that are bred to be shipped three thousand miles and survive a shelf-life measured in months. Another step might be planting a garden that grows food as well as flowers, so we may have direct experience of our covenant partner, the fertile soil.

Sure, these steps may be "only symbolic." They will not work great changes in the food industry—although consumer aversion to genetically modified food has already created a global furor where the food industrialists once expected acquiescence. But people of biblical faith have always valued symbolic (in the church, we often call it "liturgical" or "sacramental") action as a powerful help to perceiving the deepest realities, and, however gradually, bringing our lives into line with them. For many of us in this generation, good-faith eating may be the best way to practice a steady awareness that our lives are at once graced and precarious—which is to say, we depend on the generosity of God for every meal we eat. The psalmist gives us a song and prayer that tells the whole truth about us, the soil, and God's phenomenal generosity:

> Every one of them looks to you
> to give them their food at its proper time.
> You give to them; they gather it.
> You open your hand; they are filled with good.
> You hide your face; they are undone.
> You gather in their breath; they expire, and to their

dust they return.
You send your breath; they are created;
and you renew the face of the fertile soil.
Let the glory of YHWH be forever;
Let YHWH rejoice in his works—
the One who looks to the earth, and it quakes;
he touches the mountains, and they smoke.
I will sing to YHWH as long as I live;
I will make melody to my God while I have being.
                                    (Psalm 104:27-33)

It is a good song to sing at the dinner table.

Notes

1. The term derives from the form of the divine name (YHWH) that the writer employs.

2. Brother Timothy Jolley, O.H.C. This quotation originally appeared in a newsletter of the Order of the Holy Cross, West Park, New York.

3. See the NJPS *Tanakh*. The NRSV translates "to till it and keep it."

4. See Wendell Berry and Wes Jackson, eds., *Meeting the Expectations of the Land* (San Francisco: North Point Press, 1984).

5. The inclusion of the land in covenant community is supported by God's declaration following the flood: "I have set my bow in the heavens, and it will be a sign of covenant between me and the earth" (Genesis 9:13).

6. The notion that the earth should properly be reverenced is expressed thus in one contemporary prayer: "Give us all a reverence for the earth as your own creation, that we may use its resources rightly in the service of others and to your honor and glory" (BCP 388).

7. Wendell Berry, *What Are People For?* (New York: North Point Press, 1990), 209-210. Italics mine.

8. Ibid., 152.

CHAPTER SEVENTEEN

GREED AND PROPHECY

Numbers 11

Now the riffraff which was in their midst craved a craving, and indeed the Israelites wept again and said, "Who will feed us meat? We remember the fish that we used to eat in Egypt (for free!), the cucumbers, and the watermelons, and the leeks and the onions and the garlic. And now our throat is dry; nothing at all before our eyes except the manna!" (Numbers 11:4-6)

THIS CHAPTER FROM Numbers is a tangled tale of manna and quails, greed and prophecy. Israel has just left Sinai, moving through the desert like a great army on the march, and manna is falling from heaven like dew for their daily rations. But some of them are unimpressed by the bread of angels: "the riffraff" (as the writer frankly calls them) demands that God serve meat. Now, the key to this confusing story is the double answer that God gives to their gluttonous craving. First, there is the angry answer: "You want meat? I'll give you meat; you'll eat meat till it comes out your nose!"—and God pours on the quails. God's second answer is just as extravagant, but more kindly: God pours out prophecy, a spirit of prophecy so abundant that clergy and laity alike start speaking the Word of the Lord.

Unbridled greed and free-flowing prophecy—the central message of this story lies in the connection between those seeming incompatibles. It is a story that has particular importance for us who live in twenty-first century North America, because greed is the governing spirit of our society. Our craving *more than enough* is the deadly sin that is already wreaking havoc on a global scale. If we take scripture seriously, then we must believe that our greed, like Israel's, puts us in danger of God's devastating anger.

That we are greedy is indisputable. No society in the history of the world has lived as far beyond the level of subsistence as we do, and there is no doubt that the earth cannot indefinitely sustain the burden that our accustomed lifestyle imposes on it. If we are to find any hopeful message in this story (and I believe we can), it is crucial that we understand the nature of our sin, which the Christian tradition has identified as one of the seven deadliest. The essential insight on the nature of greed is found already in the Psalms. Reflecting on this story, the seventy-eighth psalm says that the Israelites demanded meat

> because they had no faith in God,
> and did not trust his saving power
> [though] he had opened the doors of heaven.
> He had rained upon them manna to eat;
> the grain of heaven he had given them.
> Mortals ate the bread of angels,
> he sent them food enough. (Psalm 78:22-25)

The psalmist goes directly to the heart of the matter: because they did not trust God, the Israelites could not be satisfied, even with the bread of angels. Greed stems always from lack of faith. We crave more than we need because we

204

do not look to God to fill the emptiness we quite accurately perceive in ourselves. In fact, *only* God can fill the emptiness within us; it is for God's sake that we alone of all the creatures are given the capacity to feel that ache of emptiness which is familiar to us all. So greed is nothing other than a perversion of our natural desire for God. Frantically and vainly we attempt to fill our emptiness with food or drink or clothes or houses or cars or works of art—with all the stuff that fills our malls and eventually our garages and garbage cans to overflowing but does not satisfy us, because it is not God. We are trying to fill ourselves with what is not God— the problem is as simple as that. Greed is simple but deadly: it kills by a kind of spiritual malnutrition. The psalmists, those brilliant spiritual diagnosticians, call it "leanness in the soul" (Psalm 106:15). False desires consume us; our souls waste away for lack of real substance.

In the biblical story, the Israelites' greed quite literally kills them. When the meat they had craved

> was still between their teeth, not yet chewed, the anger of the LORD burned hot against the people, and the LORD struck the people with a very heavy plague. And they called that place *Kivrot haTa'avah*, "Graves of Craving," for there they buried the craven people. (Numbers 11:33-34)

The great tragedy of *Kivrot haTa'avah* is that Israel already had plenty; God "sent them food enough." Manna is the great biblical symbol of sufficiency. "The grain of heaven" fell nightly for forty years in the wilderness, specifically to win Israel's trust in God and to teach them the discipline of sufficiency. In the morning each household would gather what it needed for that day and no more, for manna had no shelf life. Anyone who took more than they could use in a day ended up with a mess of maggots.

So manna in the wilderness was Israel's training in the art of sufficiency. Being content with what is enough is not just a matter of getting by, a strategy for survival in lean times until a better alternative presents itself. Rather, sufficiency is one of the chief arts of the spiritual life. Mastering any art involves practical skills but also an aesthetic sensitivity, a certain developed sense of beauty. And so with this art of sufficiency. Tuition bills, growing debt load, cutbacks at work—these things may stimulate thought about how to do with less than we have all been taught to want. But sufficiency becomes an art form only when an aesthetic change takes place within us, so that we come to see the beauty of "enough" and actually prize it over "too much."

In the Christian tradition, the great artists of sufficiency were the early monastics, the men and women who went out into the same Egyptian desert where the Israelites are traveling and camping in our story. They chose the desert specifically for its starkness, the very thing that chafed the Israelites. In the fourth century, the desert mothers and fathers were pioneering the monastic ideal of what we now call "voluntary simplicity." With typical monastic bluntness, they called their practice "mortification," literally, "making death." And in a sense, that is just what voluntary simplicity is. It is making a place in our lives for our own death.

We do it by treating our material desires always in the context of the needs of those who will come after us in this still lovely world. We make room for death by leaving the air and water as clean as we found them, by not taking more than our share of resources that can be depleted in a few generations but take geological ages to rebuild—like oil, coal, or mineral deposits, or fertile soil. The motivation for voluntary simplicity is, of course, a hunger for justice: when a few have far too much, many have too little. But also and less obviously, it is *aesthetically* motivated. Excessive consumption is ugly, as Numbers graphically displays: the Israelites are wading in quail up to their armpits, stuffing themselves until the meat comes out their nostrils. This picture is meant to be repellant. It is a sad irony that, craving a superabundance of stuff in order to magnify our worth, we are actually diminished in our dignity—certainly in God's eyes and, if we are observant, in our own.

The biblical story is deeply disturbing, but it also affords an element of chastened hope. The hope lies in God's second extravagant answer to Israel's greed, when God pours out a spirit of prophecy that more than fills the seventy officially appointed elders. The overflow of prophetic spirit runs out into the camp of ordinary Israelites, so that two guys named Eldad and Medad start speaking God's truth. And when Joshua son of Nun complains that things have gotten out of hand, Moses says, "What, are you jealous for me? If only all God's people were prophets!"

So what is the connection between Israel's greed and this overflow of prophecy? We are not told the content of the prophecy, so we have to guess. But we know this: the basic function of all the prophets is to give Israel a God's-eye view of its situation—to help the people see when what they are doing is hostile to God and call them back to a life lived in dignity and beauty before God. And so here at the Graves of Craving, I imagine the prophets were trying to reorient the people from craving for meat to gratitude for manna. In no uncertain terms they challenged Israel to focus on God's faithfulness instead of their own wants.

And what does this have to do with us? At the risk of sounding weird, I believe that in our time we are experiencing a similar overflow of prophecy, for God's truth is being uttered in startling and compelling ways even by Eldad and Medad—that is, by people whom the church has not officially charged to speak for God. Catholic Christianity is rightly wary of identifying people outside the Bible as prophets, but in this instance the biblical story itself pushes us to this kind of language: "If only all God's people were prophets!"

Various people in our society are performing the prophetic task of waking us up to our hostility toward God and God's creation. I am thinking of the economists who point to the fact that our nation, with six percent of the world's population, presently uses thirty-five percent of its resources—six times our fair share; or the political analysts who show the connection between international violence and our own gluttonous craving for gasoline, plastics, and other petroleum products. Another function of the biblical prophets is to speak on behalf of the poor: those people, generally invisible to us, who suffer because of our selfishness. If we read the daily news in light of their prophecy, we will recognize with increasing clarity that our lifestyle extracts a price from people most of us will never see in person, at least this side of the Resurrection. Third World countries have little to sell on the global market but the bones of their land—its minerals and forests—and the cheap labor of their people. They are exchanging short-term gain for ever deepening long-term poverty as their land is stripped and their water and air are polluted, in no small part by First World industries.

More shocking to us, the invisible people who suffer from our selfishness include our own grandchildren and great-grandchildren, who will live on soil presently being worn out by high-chemical, maximum-production agriculture. They will drink water from rivers, lakes, and bays that are dumping grounds for industrial chemicals and toxic sewage. The most startling prophetic proclamation of our time is that the earth itself suffers on account of our selfishness. One theologian calls the earth and its non-human inhabitants "the new poor." All over the globe the God-given richness of the natural world is being diminished; plant and animal species are becoming extinct more rapidly than at any time since the Ice Age as their natural habitats are poisoned, unnaturally warmed, paved over, or clear-cut.

We do not normally talk about this in church—or in seminaries, for that matter. Like Joshua son of Nun, the church has not on the whole been eager to recognize the unordained prophets who speak the truth in this matter. But Moses says to Joshua, "What, are you jealous for me? If only all God's people were prophets!" I challenge you, as a spiritual discipline, to take up the prophetic task of identifying the connection—the myriad small connections—between what we do and the well-being of God's creation. I warn you now that drawing those connections is painful; it means choosing to see the deep woundedness of the world and our own complicity in inflicting those wounds.

The church has been too slow to name the healing of the earth as a central Christian responsibility. Nonetheless, this is the best place for us to stand—within the church—as we struggle to meet that responsibility. For Christian worship itself is basic training in the art of sufficiency. Here we learn to ask for what is enough for us: "Give us this day our daily bread." Here we receive the one thing that can truly satisfy us, the bread of heaven, that draws our memory back to manna in the wilderness—when, against all the odds, everyone had enough, riffraff included. The liturgy points our imagination forward to the heavenly banquet where all will be filled, riffraff included. So listen carefully to the language of the eucharist. Every prayer is teaching us to speak the language of sufficiency, to articulate, and gradually, if we allow ourselves, to feel the consummate satisfaction of those who feed on Christ in their hearts by faith, with thanksgiving. Come then, the table is ready. Eat, and be filled. Drink deeply, and be satisfied. Amen.

Cowley Publications is a ministry of the Society of St. John the Evangelist, a religious community for men in the Episcopal Church. Emerging from the Society's tradition of prayer, theological reflection, and diversity of mission, the press is centered in the rich heritage of the Anglican Communion.

Cowley Publications seeks to provide books, CDs, audio cassettes, and other resources for the ongoing theological exploration and spiritual development of the Episcopal Church and others in the body of Christ. To this end, it is dedicated to developing a new generation of theological writers, encouraging them to produce timely, creative, and stimulating publications of excellence, and making these publications available widely, reaching both clergy and lay persons.